On *The Revival of the Religious Sciences* (*Iḥyāʾ ʿulūm al-dīn*)

"The *Iḥyāʾ ʿulūm al-dīn* is the most valuable and most beautiful of books."
—Aḥmad b. Muḥammad Ibn Khallikān (d. 681/1282)

"The *Iḥyāʾ ʿulūm al-dīn* is one of al-Ghazālī's best works."
—Aḥmad b. ʿAbd al-Ḥalīm (d. 728/1328)

"Any seeker of [felicity of] the hereafter cannot do without the *Iḥyāʾ ʿulūm al-dīn*"
—ʿAbd al-Wahhāb b. ʿAlī l-Subkī (d. 771/1370)

"The *Iḥyāʾ ʿulūm al-dīn* is a marvelous book containing a wide variety of Islamic sciences intermixed with many subtle accounts of Sufism and matters of the heart."
—Ismāʿīl b. ʿUmar Ibn Kathīr (d. 774/1373)

"The *Iḥyāʾ ʿulūm al-dīn* is one of best and greatest books on admonition, it was said concerning it, 'if all the books of Islam were lost except for the *Iḥyāʾ* it would suffice what was lost.'"
—Musṭafā b. ʿAbdallāh Ḥājjī Khalīfa Kātib Čelebī (d. 1067/1657)

"The *Iḥyāʾ [ʿulūm al-dīn]* is one of [Imām al-Ghazālī's] most noble works, his most famous work, and by far his greatest work'"
—Muḥammad b. Muḥammad Murtaḍā l-Zabīdī (d. 1205/1791)

On Imām al-Ghazālī

"Al-Ghazālī is [like] a deep ocean [of knowledge]."

—ʿAbd al-Malik b. ʿAbdallāh al-Juwaynī (d. 478/1085)

"Abū Ḥāmid al-Ghazālī, the Proof of Islam (Ḥujjat al-Islām) and the Muslims, the Imām of the imāms of religion, [is a man] whose like has not been seen in eloquence and elucidation, in speech and thought, and in acumen and natural ability."

—ʿAbd al-Ghāfir b. Ismāʿīl al-Fārisī (d. 529/1134)

"Al-Ghazālī is the second [Imām] Shāfiʿī."

—Muḥammad b. Yaḥyā l-Janzī (d. 549/1154)

"[He was] the Proof of Islam and Muslims, Imām of the imāms of religious sciences, one of vast knowledge, the wonder of the ages, the author of many works, and [a man] of extreme intelligence and the best of the sincere."

—Muḥammad b. ʿUthmān al-Dhahabī (d. 748/1347)

"Al-Ghazālī is without doubt the most remarkable figure in all Islam."

—T.J. DeBoer (d. 1942)

". . . A man who stands on a level with Augustine and Luther in religious insight and intellectual vigor."

—H.A.R. Gibb (d. 1971)

"I have to some extent found, and I believe others can find, in the words and example of al-Ghazālī a true *iḥyāʾ* . . ."

—Richard J. McCarthy, S.J. (d. 1981)

The Forty Books of
The Revival of the Religious Sciences
(*Iḥyāʾ ʿulūm al-dīn*)

The Quarter of Worship

1 The Book of Knowledge
2 The Principles of the Creed
3 The Mysteries of Purification
4 The Mysteries of the Prayer
5 The Mysteries of Charity
6 The Mysteries of Fasting
7 The Mysteries of the Pilgrimage
8 The Etiquette of the Recitation of the Qurʾān
9 Invocations and Supplications
10 The Arrangement of the Litanies and the Exposition of the Night Vigil

The Quarter of Customs

11 The Proprieties of Eating
12 The Proprieties of Marriage
13 The Proprieties of Acquisition and Earning a Living
14 The Lawful and the Unlawful
15 The Proprieties of Friendship and Brotherhood
16 The Proprieties of Retreat
17 The Proprieties of Travel
18 The Proprieties of the Audition and Ecstasy
19 The Commanding of Right and the Forbidding of Wrong
20 Prophetic Ethics and the Courtesies of Living

The Quarter of Perils

21 The Exposition of the Wonders of the Heart
22 Training the Soul, Refining the Character, and Treating the Ailments of the Heart
23 Overcoming the Two Desires
24 The Bane of the Tongue
25 The Censure of Anger, Malice, and Envy
26 The Censure of This World
27 The Censure of Greed and the Love of Wealth
28 The Censure of Fame and Hypocritical Ostentation
29 The Censure of Pride and Vanity
30 The Censure of Deceit

The Quarter of Deliverance

31 On Repentance
32 On Patience and Thankfulness
33 On Fear and Hope
34 On Poverty and Abstinence
35 On Unity and Trust
36 On Love, Longing, Intimacy, and Contentment
37 On Intention, Sincerity, and Truthfulness
38 On Vigilance and Accounting
39 On Contemplation
40 On the Remembrance of Death and the Hereafter

THE BOOK OF PROPHETIC ETHICS AND THE COURTESIES OF LIVING

Kitāb Ādāb al-maʿīsha wa-akhlāq al-nubuwwa

Book 20 of

The Revival of the Religious Sciences

Iḥyāʾ ʿulūm al-dīn

بسم الله الرحمن الرحيم

AL-GHAZĀLĪ

Kitāb Ādāb al-maʿīsha wa-akhlāq al-nubuwwa

THE BOOK OF PROPHETIC ETHICS AND THE COURTESIES OF LIVING

Book 20 of the *Iḥyāʾ ʿulūm al-dīn*

THE REVIVAL OF THE RELIGIOUS SCIENCES

Translated *from the* Arabic
with an Introduction *and* Notes

by Adi Setia

Fons Vitae
2019

Prophetic Ethics and the Courtesies of Living, Book 20 of
The Revival of the Religious Sciences, first published in 2019 by

Fons Vitae
49 Mockingbird Valley Drive
Louisville, KY 40207 USA

www.fonsvitae.com

The Fons Vitae Ghazali Series
Library of Congress Control Number: 2018956346
ISBN 978-1941610-428

Book design: Muhammad Hozien
Text typeface: Adobe Minion Pro 11/13.5
Editing and indexing: Neville Blakemore, Jr.

Translation of Shaykh Ninowy's Introduction by Nancy Roberts

Cover art courtesy the of National Library of Egypt, Cairo.
Qurʾānic frontispiece to part 19. Written and illuminated by ʿAbdallāh b.
Muḥammad al-Ḥamadānī for Sultan Uljaytu 713/1313. Hamadan.

Printed in Canada

Contents

Biography of Imām al-Ghazālī xi

Preface xvii
Foreword xxi
Introduction xxiii
Translator's Introduction xxxix

The Book of Prophetic Ethics and the Courtesies of Living 1

Author's Introduction 3

Chapter 1
An Account of the Refinement by God Most High of His Beloved and Chosen, Muḥammad 7

Chapter 2
An Account of a Portion of His Nobilities of Ethical Character That Have Been Brought Together by Some of the Scholars and Assembled from the Reports 13

Chapter 3
An Account of Some Other Aspects of His Comportment and Character 21

Chapter 4
An Account of His Speech and Laughter 27

Chapter 5
An Account of His Ethics and Comportment in Regard to Food 31

Chapter 6
An Account of His Manners and Character in Regard to Attire 37

Chapter 7
An Account of His Forgiveness Notwithstanding His Ability to Censure 43

Chapter 8
An Account of His Averting of His Gaze from Whatever He Disliked 47

Chapter 9
An Account of His Munificence and Generosity 49

Chapter 10
An Account of His Bravery........ 51

Chapter 11
An Account of His Humility 53

Chapter 12
An Account of His External Manner and Countenance 57

Chapter 13
An Account of His Miracles and Signs Indicative of His Truthfulness 61

Bibliography 71

Indices
Index of Qurʾānic Verses........ 76
Index of *Ḥadīth*........ 77
Index of People........ 82
Index of Places 84
Index of Subjects 85

About the Translator 89
About the Author of the Preface 90
About the Author of the Foreword 91
About the Author of the Introduction 92

Biography of Imām al-Ghazālī

He is Abū Ḥāmid Muḥammad b. Muḥammad b. Muḥammad b. Aḥmad al-Ghazālī l-Ṭūsī; he was born in 450/1058 in the village of Ṭābarān near Ṭūs (in northeast Iran) and he died there, at the age of fifty-five, in 505/1111. Muḥammad's father died when he and his younger brother Aḥmad were still young; their father left a little money for their education in the care of a Sufi friend of limited means. When the money ran out, their caretaker suggested that they enroll in a *madrasa*. The *madrasa* system meant they had a stipend, room, and board. Al-Ghazālī studied *fiqh* in his hometown under a Sufi named Aḥmad al-Rādhakānī; he then traveled to Jurjān and studied under Ismāʿīl b. Masʿada al-Ismāʿīlī (d. 477/1084).

On his journey home his caravan was overtaken by highway robbers who took all of their possessions. Al-Ghazālī went to the leader of the bandits and demanded his notebooks. The leader asked, "What are these notebooks?" Al-Ghazālī answered, "This is the knowledge that I traveled far to acquire." The leader acquiesced to al-Ghazālī's demands after stating, "If you claim that it is knowledge that you have, how can we take it away from you?" This incident left a lasting impression on the young scholar. Thereafter, he returned to Ṭūs for three years, where he committed to memory all that he had learned thus far.

In 469/1077 he traveled to Nīsābūr to study with the leading scholar of his time, Imām al-Ḥaramayn al-Juwaynī (d. 478/1085), at the Niẓāmiyya College. He remained his student for approximately eight years, until al-Juwaynī died. Al-Ghazālī was one of his most illustrious students, and al-Juwaynī referred to him as "a deep ocean [of knowledge]." As one of al-Juwaynī's star pupils, al-Ghazālī used to fill in as a substitute lecturer in his teacher's absence. He also tutored his fellow students in the subjects that al-Juwaynī taught at the Niẓāmiyya. Al-Ghazālī wrote his first book, on the founding principles of legal theory (*uṣūl al-fiqh*), while studying with al-Juwaynī.

Very little is known about al-Ghazālī's family, though some biographers mention that he married while in Nīsābūr; others note that he had married in Ṭūs prior to leaving for Nīsābūr. Some accounts state that he had five children, a son who died early and four daughters. Accounts also indicate that his mother lived to see her son rise to fame and fortune.

After the death of al-Juwaynī, al-Ghazālī went to the camp (*al-muʿaskar*) of the Saljūq *wazīr* Niẓām al-Mulk (d. 485/1192). He stayed at the camp, a gathering place for scholars, and quickly distinguished himself among their illustrious company. Niẓām al-Mulk recognized al-Ghazālī's genius and appointed him professor at the famed Niẓāmiyya College of Baghdad.

Al-Ghazālī left for Baghdad in 484/1091 and stayed there four years—it was a very exciting time to be in the heart of the Islamic empire. At the Niẓāmiyya College he had many students, by some estimates as many as three hundred. In terms of his scholarly output, this was also a prolific period in which he wrote *Maqāṣid al-falāsifa, Tahāfut al-falāsifa, al-Mustaẓhirī,* and other works.

Al-Ghazālī was well connected politically and socially; there is evidence that he settled disputes related to the legitimacy of the rule of the ʿAbbāsid caliph, al-Mustaẓhir (r. 487–512/1094–1118), who assumed his role as caliph when he was just fifteen years old, after the death of his father al-Muqtadī (d. 487/1094). Al-Ghazālī issued a *fatwā* of approval of the appointment of al-Mustaẓhir and was present at the oath-taking ceremony.

In Baghdad, al-Ghazālī underwent a spiritual crisis during which he was overcome by fear of the punishment of Hell. He became convinced that he was destined for Hell if he did not change his ways; he feared that he had become too engrossed in worldly affairs to the detriment of his spiritual being. He began to question his true intentions: was he writing and teaching to serve God, or because he enjoyed the fame and fortune that resulted from his lectures. He experienced much suffering, both inward and outward; one day as he stood before his students to present a lecture, he found himself unable to speak. The physicians were unable to diagnose any physical malady. Al-Ghazālī remained in Baghdad for a time, then left his teaching post for the pilgrimage. He left behind fortune, fame, and influence. He was beloved by his numerous students and had many admirers, including the sultan; he was also envied by many. The presumption is that he left in the manner he did—ostensibly to undertake the pilgrimage—because if he had made public his intention to leave permanently, those around him would have tried to convince him to remain and the temptation might have been too strong to resist.

After leaving Baghdad, he changed direction and headed toward Damascus; according to his autobiography he disappeared from the intellectual scene for ten years. This does not mean that he did not teach, but that he did not want to return to public life and be paid for teaching. This ten-year period can be divided into two phases. First, he spent two years in the East—in greater Syria, where most of his time was spent in Damascus. He went on the Hajj and also spent time in Jerusalem. From time to time, he visited his family who may have been in Iraq. It's during this period that he wrote the famed *Iḥyāʾ ʿulūm al-dīn*, a work that was inspired by his change of outlook resulting from his spiritual crisis. When that period was over (10 years from the time he gave up his post at the Nizamiyya in Baghdad), he then went back to Ṭūs for good.

When he arrived back in his hometown in 490/1097, he established a school and a Sufi lodge in order to continue teaching and learning. In 499/1106, Niẓām al-Mulk's son, Fakhr al-Mulk, requested that al-Ghazālī accept a teaching position at his old school, the Niẓāmiyya of Nīsābūr. He accepted and taught for a time, but left this position in 500/1106 after Fakhr al-Mulk was assassinated by Ismāʿīlīs. He then returned to Ṭūs and divided his time between teaching and worship. He died in 505/1111 and was buried in a cemetery near the citadel of Ṭābarān.

Legacy and Contributions of al-Ghazālī

Al-Ghazālī's two hundred and seventy-three works span many disciplines and can be grouped under the following headings:

1. Jurisprudence and legal theory. Al-Ghazālī made foundational contributions to Shāfiʿī jurisprudence; his book *al-Wajīz* is a major handbook that has been used in teaching institutions around the world; many commentaries have been written on it, most notably by Abū l-Qāsim ʿAbd al-Karīm al-Rāfiʿī (d. 623/1226). In legal theory, *al-Mustaṣfa min ʿilm al-uṣūl* is considered one of five foundational texts in the discipline.
2. Logic and philosophy. Al-Ghazālī introduced logic in Islamic terms that jurists could understand and utilize. His works on philosophy include the *Tahāfut al-falāsifa*, which has been studied far beyond the Muslim world and has been the subject of numerous commentaries, discussions, and refutations.
3. Theology, including works on heresiography in refutation of Bāṭinī doctrines. He also expounded on the theory of occasionalism.
4. Ethics and educational theory. The *Mīzān al-ʿamal* and other works such as the *Iḥyāʾ ʿulūm al-dīn* mention a great deal on education.
5. Spirituality and Sufism. His magnum opus, the *Iḥyāʾ ʿulūm al-dīn* is a pioneering work in the field of spirituality, in terms of its organization and its comprehensive scope.
6. Various fields. Al-Ghazālī also wrote shorter works in a variety of disciplines, including his autobiography (*al-Munqidh min al-ḍalāl*), works on Qurʾānic studies (*Jawāhir al-Qurʾān*), and political statecraft (*Naṣiḥat al-mūluk*).

Chronology of al-Ghazālī's Life

450/1058	Birth of al-Ghazālī in Ṭūs
c. 461/1069	Began studies in Ṭūs
c. 465/1073	Traveled to Jurjān to study
466–469/1074–1077	Studied in Ṭūs
469/1077	Studied with al-Jūwaynī at the Niẓāmiyya college in Nīsābūr
473/1080	Composed his first book, *al-Mankhūl fī l-uṣūl*
477/1084	Death of al-Fāramdhī, one of al-Ghazālī's teachers
25 Rabīʿ II 478/ 20 August 1085	Death of al-Jūwaynī; al-Ghazālī left Nīsābūr
Jumāda I 484/ July 1091	Appointed to teach at the Niẓāmiyya college in Baghdad
10 Ramaḍān 485/ 14 October 1092	Niẓām-al-Mulk was assassinated
484–487/1091–1094	Studied philosophy
Muḥarrām 487/ February 1094	Attended the oath-taking of the new caliph, al-Mustaẓhir
487/1094	Finished *Maqāṣid al-falāsifa*
5 Muḥarrām 488/ 21 January 1095	Finished *Tahāfut al-falāsifa*
Rajab 488/ July 1095	Experienced a spiritual crisis
Dhū l-Qaʿda 488/ November 1095	Left Baghdad for Damascus
Dhū l-Qaʿda 489/ November – December 1096	Made pilgrimage and worked on the *Iḥyāʾ ʿulūm al-dīn*
Jumāda II 490/ May 1097	Taught from the *Iḥyāʾ ʿulūm al-dīn* during a brief stop in Baghdad
Rajab 490/June 1097	Seen in Baghdad by Abū Bakr b. al-ʿArabī
Fall 490/1097	Returned to Ṭūs

Dhū l-Ḥijja 490/ November 1097	Established a *madrasa* and a *khānqāh* in Ṭūs
Dhū l-Qaʿda 499/ July 1106	Taught at the Niẓāmiyya college in Nīsābūr
500/1106	Wrote *al-Munqidh min al-ḍalāl*
500/1106	Returned to Ṭūs
28 Dhū l-Ḥijja 502/ 5 August 1109	Finished *al-Mustaṣfā min ʿilm al-uṣūl*
Jumada I 505/ December 1111	Finished *Iljām al-ʿawām ʿan ʿilm al-kalām*
14 Jumada II 505/ 18 December 1111	Died in Ṭūs

Eulogies in Verse

> Because of him the lame walked briskly,
> And the songless through him burst into melody.

On the death of Imām al-Ghazālī, Abū l-Muẓaffar Muḥammad al-Abiwardī said of his loss:

> He is gone! and the greatest loss which ever afflicted me,
> was that of a man who left no one like him among mankind.

Preface

by Shaykh Walead Mohammed Mosaad

BOOK XX, *Prophetic Ethics and the Courtesies of Living*, represents the heart of the whole of al-Ghazali's *magnum opus*. If the *dīn* is comprised of *adāb* (comportment and proprieties), as the Prophet Muḥammad ﷺ stated: "I have not been sent except to perfect the nobility of character", then one would have to conclude that comportment and etiquette require prophetic and divine guidance to perfect, and is not, as some of the philosophers, both ancient and modern have surmised, a merely rational exercise. That one must simply put one's mind to it, and beautiful traits should ensue – rings hollow, as one need not look further than one's self to see the absurdity of such an assertion. Modern people are inundated daily with claims for happiness were they only to follow, for example, the latest trendy diet, or "research" on human happiness. Yet, despite the plethora and cacophony of the daily stream of advice for a better life, the *better* life, nonetheless, remains elusive for most.

Religion has been largely dismissed as a source for general welfare and happiness by both the irreligious as well as some of those committed to a faith tradition. Religion often retreats to the confines of identity politics or to a sort of religious and sectarian tribalism, echoing the general contemporary trend in politics, business, and social relationships. As a result, the world eerily descends towards a complete loss of meaning in everything that ever was meaningful.

Most are oblivious to this very occurrence.

It is our assertion that the root cause of this state of affairs is the loss of *adāb*, the sum of the personal, communal, and societal courtesies of living and etiquette in the Islamic tradition, as taught, practiced and actualized by the Prophet Muḥammad ﷺ. Some of the *ulama* have asserted that these character traits exemplified by the Prophet Muḥammad ﷺ are enough to provide certainty for the claim of his prophethood, as they can not be found in any other human being to such a level of perfection. He ﷺ was the most devoted husband and father, the most forgiving companion and confidant, the most courageous leader, the most giving friend, and the most worshipful servant of God. Furthermore, he was able to exemplify these beautiful character traits for his companions to such a degree of embodiment and perfection that they too were also able to pass them on to their companions, and thereafter to the Muslims of the present day. This represents the inherited wisdom tradition of Islam, that is not merely passed on through books and texts, but rather also through living and breathing inheritors of the grace, spiritual fortitude, and all-encompassing beauty of the Prophet Muḥammad ﷺ.

The importance of this Prophetic beauty, though in the eyes of some seeming only to constitute mere minutiae, was not lost on the companions of the Messenger of God ﷺ. They recorded the number of gray hairs observed in his beard, as well as the way his hand felt upon its touch. They recorded his interactions with his family, even the manner by which he combed his hair, and his gentle words to a distraught young boy who had lost his pet sparrow. They recorded his readiness to take a ring to be a seal on his official letters when informed that foreign rulers would otherwise not accept them. They recorded the flow of his tears when he buried his son, Ibrahim. Perhaps the best summation of these reports is the remark of 'Alī ibn Abī Ṭālib, the cousin and son-in-law of the Prophet Muḥammad ﷺ, proclaiming that he never saw any one before or after him like the noble Prophet ﷺ.

Other religious traditions certainly emphasize the importance of many of these same manners, but arguably none of them have produced such detailed and precise records of their chief exemplar's exploits, nor have any of them produced such a prolific and rich tradition of scholarly work on their prophet's moral and ethical imperatives. Al-Ghazālī is not the first to present these beautiful traits and examples of what humanity ought to be, but his summation, included as the twentieth pivotal volume in the *Iḥyā'*, forms the centerpiece of the whole work. If the *Iḥyā'* is a work of moral instruction and ethics, then not including a book dedicated to the one who is an embodiment of all that is pristine, beautiful, and saintly in human form, would be remiss. In this, Imam al-Ghazālī succeeds, as he most often does, by presenting the reader with a thorough analysis of Islam's most defining characteristic – the exemplary inner and outer beauty of its Prophet and Messenger ﷺ.

He is the oft-praised one, Muḥammad in the earthly realm
And Ahmad as he is known by those who command the angelic helm
He is the one sent by his Lord as a mercy to all
To every creature, rock, sea, sparrow, and mistral
He is the one whose intercession is desired by the pious and all trespassers
"Myself Myself!" – the refrain of all others, but as creation swelters
He is the one who is the delight of our eyes and the courage of our wit
Proclaiming when all seemed lost, I am the one for it!
He is the one who took the Quran as his character
Compassionate, wise, and gentle, knowing no anger
Except in matters where Providence's boundaries were crossed
But even then his inner beauty and luster were never lost
All told, the world would not have been, save for God's favor
By sending His messenger the most noble of saviors
Praise Him much and implore Him to offer His blessings and salutations
On the best of all creation whose virtue
Made us the best of all nations!

Shaykh Walead Mohammed Mosaad
Bethlehem, Pennsylvania
17 Jumada II 1440
21 February 2019

Foreword

by Shaykh Dato' Dr. Afifi al-Akiti

ONE of Imām al-Ghazālī's timeless aphorisms can be found in this feather-light yet brimming tome from the *Iḥyāʾ ʿUlūm al-Dīn*:

> Our external etiquette (or manners) is but an indicator of our internal comportment *(ādāb al ẓawāhir ʿunwān ādāb al-bawāṭin).*

Indeed, this is a bedrock law of nature, a divine custom, of how the Creator programmed His creation: that one's morals direct one's behavior, and never the other way round. The *Kitāb Ādāb al-Maʿīsha wa-Akhlāq al-Nubuwwa (The Book of Prophetic Ethics and the Courtesies of Living)* by the Ḥujjat al-Islām al-Ghazālī is indeed an amazing code of the Almighty's most perfect creation, penned on a mere few pages in simple language. It is one of the most unique *Ḥilya*s ever written to portray the Muslim Prophet (may God's peace and blessings be upon him).

Al-Ghazālī portrayed most accurately the comportment expected of the Perfect Man (*Insān al-kāmil*): theoretically rigorous and congruent in its depiction, as already scattered throughout the *Iḥyāʾ*. At precisely this halfway point, at the very heart of his *magnum opus*, it is portrayed as collating and revealing a paragon for mankind that is both stunning and stirring in its practical import. Hence, it handily becomes an accessible compact guide for leading our lives by emulating this perfect being as our role model.

The work that lies open before us is the latest English translation of al-Ghazālī's *Ḥilya*, Book XX of the *Iḥyāʾ*. In this endeavor, Dr. Adi Setia has carefully and methodically rendered the original eloquent prose of the great Imām into an equally accessible text for modern-day readers, while striking a fine balance between scholarly rigor and a reader-friendly format in documentation. Let us all invoke the fitting, concluding prayers offered by al-Ghazālī himself:

> How great indeed is the success of those who have believed in him, affirmed his truthfulness and followed him in all matters. We beseech God Most High to grant us facilitation in emulating him in his character, deeds, conduct and sayings, through His bestowal and ample munificence! *Amin!*

May God Most Gracious facilitate for us the trodden path to emulating His Beloved through reading and taking benefit from this simple yet profound work! *Amin*!

Shaykh Dato' Dr. Afifi al-Akiti
Oxford University and
Orang Besar 8 Perak of Malaysia
27 Rajab 1439
14 April 2018

Introduction
In Praise

by Shaykh Muhammad Bin Yahya al-Ninowy

In the Name of God, Most Compassionate, Most Merciful

PRAISE be to God, Whose majesty no language or thought can encompass, to Whom nothing can be likened, Whose luminous emanations dazzle heart and soul, the light of Whose knowledge illumines the eye, outer and inner alike, the knowledge of Whose mysteries penetrates the thickest of veils, Who perceives the most hidden and subtle of realities, the Knower of the deceits of the soul and the realities buried deep in the conscience, Who stands in no need of any other and of Whom all others stand in need, the Turner of hearts and Forgiver of sins, the Concealer of faults, the Alleviator of calamities, the Treasure of every loving heart.

May blessing and abundant peace be upon the light of lights, the mystery of mysteries, the antidote to worldly concerns and preoccupations, the beloved healer, our master Muḥammad, the chosen Prophet, and upon his noble, pure-hearted wives and righteous companions.

And now to our topic.

God Almighty has honored human beings with the capacity for choice, thereby equipping them for nearness, intimacy, knowledge and illumination with the light of God, be He praised and exalted, the Most Generous of the Generous and the Most Forgiving of the Forgiving. The predisposition to know the Maker and Sovereign of all the worlds resides in the heart. The heart can be replaced by neither reason nor opportunity, nor can the effulgence of the divine light be received via the intellect. Rather, the heart is the portal to the knowledge of God Almighty. It is the heart that draws near to God. It is the heart that labors for God. It is the heart that journeys to God, that strives for God, that searches for God, that acquires understanding of God. The heart is the locus of the vision of God, the faculty that receives revelations concerning what abides in the presence of God. As for our bodily members, they are subordinate instruments which are used by the mind and the heart in accordance with one's propensities, and the degree of power exercised by the mind or the heart over one's thoughts, words and actions. The heart nearest and most acceptable to God is the heart that is filled with God alone and which sees nothing and no one but God. Conversely, the heart most distant from God and the least able to perceive God due to the veil placed upon it, is the heart which, immersed in the affairs of this material world, is preoccupied with that which is not God. Such a heart sees the gift of grace but not its Giver. It is the heart that is addressed by the divine speech and called upon to act on this speech. Similarly, it is that heart that is chastised, awakened to God's vibrant love, drawn near and called to account under the ever-vigilant divine eye.

When purified, the heart finds delight in the spiritual stations of nearness to God Almighty, but when tainted by impurity, it suffers wretchedness and infirmity. When the heart obeys God Almighty in that which is true, the actions, words and thoughts expressed via the limbs, the tongue and the mind reflect the light of its guidance. And when, conversely, the heart disobeys and rebels against the truth it has received from God Almighty, the resulting actions, thoughts and words are the fruits of its darkness. The heart is our innermost being, our core. When the inner being is sound, so is the outer; conversely, when the interior is rotten, so will be the exterior. Our outer beings will be beautiful or ugly depending on the light or darkness that prevails in our hearts. A vessel exudes that which it contains. She who knows her own heart knows herself, and she who knows herself knows her Lord. Conversely, she who is ignorant of her own heart is ignorant of herself, and she who is ignorant of herself is ignorant of her Lord. Those who are heedless of their own hearts will be still more heedless of others'; and those who are ignorant of their own hearts will be even more ignorant of others'.

Most people are, in fact, heedless of themselves. Neglectful of their true nature and oblivious to their hearts, they have forgotten God, and God has forgotten them. Veils now hang between them and their own souls, woven by their heedlessness and the distances they have traversed through spiritual slumber. Their obliviousness to themselves stands as a barrier between them and their hearts, preventing them from drawing near to and loving God Almighty, and from recognizing their inner poverty by coming into God's presence through prayer, humble entreaty, and supplication. However, their initial flight from God may become a flight to Him, whereupon they see God with the eye of the heart and appreciate His watchful, ever-present scrutiny. On one occasion one might see the heart sink to such depths of depravity that it joins the ranks of the demons, while on another occasion, it will rise to such heights of sublimity that it reaches the realm of the Spirit, the Kingdom of Heaven, and the abode of the angels brought near. In short, knowledge of the heart and how to train it is the foundation of this religion and the basis of the believer's path. These are life's fundamental truths, the paths followed by God's messengers and prophets, and the rules of conduct to which they adhered on their journeys.

By God's grace, Imām al-Ghazālī's *The Revival of the Religious Sciences* has succeeded in occupying people's minds and hearts the world over since the lifetime of al-Ghazālī himself (450-505 AH/1058-1111 CE) to this very day. Reactions to his work have ranged from loving welcome and praise, to hostile detraction and denunciation. Al-Ghazālī mentioned three purposes for his having penned this work. The first, as the title indicates, was to revive the sciences of religion, that is, to breathe new life into the disciplines dealing with the teachings of Islam. The need for such a revival lay in the fact that people had turned their religion into little more than information to be memorized, litanies to be repeated, and garments or titles which, by clothing oneself in them, one hoped to achieve personal gain, and acquire prominence over associates and rivals. The second purpose of the book was to identify the sciences that had been established and pursued by the leading early Muslim scholars. The third purpose was to clarify and explain those sciences which are of benefit to human beings in both this world and the next, viewing the knowledge acquired through them as a means rather than as an end, as a tool rather than as a motive force, as a sign of progress toward a goal rather than the goal itself.

There are growing demands for Muslims to engage in innovative interpretations and to modernize religious thought as a means of confronting the organized atheistic extremism which is spreading throughout the world's societies. At the same time, there has been a concerted attack on the system of ethical and humanitarian values shared by the world's religions. Further, there is ongoing pressure to find a swift-acting remedy for the phenomenon of intellectual, verbal and physical violence, and effective responses to the claims of intellectual superiority and supremacy being made by certain influential Islamic groups. Nevertheless, Imām al-Ghazālī continues to be a rich source of inspiration for modern reformers despite the passage of nearly a thousand years since his death.

One reason for al-Ghazālī's ongoing relevance is the fact that he witnessed conditions that bear numerous resemblances to those that face us today. In the face of the circumstances that prevailed in his time, al-Ghazālī deposited the essence of his thought in *The Revival of the Religious Sciences*, a comprehensive work in which he brought together the three religious foundations of doctrine, legal rulings and morals. In so doing, his purpose was to manifest the dimensions of charity, inward purification, love and the heart's relationship to God in all aspects of life in order to promote human advancement in the realms of thought, speech and action alike. His dream was to see words translated into meanings, suggestions into verbal and physical expressions, and statements into genuine revival and awakening in thought, word and deed.

References to Imām al-Ghazālī have adorned many a book, and on him many an honorific title has been conferred. He has been known variously as *Hujjat al-Islām (Proof of Islam), Zayn al-Dīn (Adornment of the Religion), Nāsir al-Dīn (Protector of the Religion),*

Muḥyī ʿUlūm al-Dīn (Reviver of the Sciences of Religion), al-Mujaddid (The Renewer), al-Faqīh (The Jurist), al-Ṣūfī (The Mystic), al-Uṣūlī (Master of Islamic Legal Theory), al-Naẓẓār al-Tawḥīdī al-Mutakallim (The Keen-Eyed Scholar of the Oneness of the Divine), al-Faylasūf (The Philosopher), al-Qāḍī (The Judge), and al-Wāʿiz (The Preacher). In his biographical compendium entitled *Siyar Aʿlām al-Nubalāʾ (Biographies of Noble Luminaries),*[1] al-Ḥāfiẓ al-Dhahabī described al-Ghazālī as "*al-Bahr (The Sea of Knowledge), Ḥujjat al-Islām (The Proof of Islam), Uʿjūbat al-Zamān (Wonder of the Age), Zayn al-Dīn (Adornment of the Religion),* Abū Ḥāmid Muḥammad Bin Muḥammad Bin Aḥmad al-Ṭūsī al-Shāfiʿī al-Ghazālī, author of countless tomes and boundless genius." Similarly, he was described by al-Subkī in his biographical dictionary of Shāfiʿī scholars entitled *Tabaqāt al-Shāfiʿiyah al-Kubrā*[2] as "*Ḥujjat al-Islām (The Proof of Islam),* the one who gathered the scattered pieces of the Islamic sciences that had come down to us and shed upon them the light of understanding."

The great Shāfiʿī Ashʿarī jurist Imām al-Ghazālī with the mystic bent was born in Khurasan to a spinner of humble means, and grew up in a poor household. It appears that al-Ghazālī's father was so destitute that he sent his son to study in a school that sponsored the educations of indigent and orphaned children and provided them with food as well. It wasn't long before the boy began showing signs of exceptional intelligence, and it is said that the Shāfiʿī scholar Abū al-Maʿālī al-Juwaynī (d. 478 AH/1085 CE) once quipped to the young al-Ghazālī, "Do you intend to slay me alive?! Would that you had had the patience to wait until I perished of my own accord!"

In his book, *al-Munqidh min al-Ḍalāl (Deliverance from Error),* al-Ghazālī introduced himself with the words,

> Should I encounter a Bāṭinī, I would want to familiarize myself with his Bāṭinī beliefs. When I meet a Ẓāhirī, I strive to know where his Ẓāhirī convictions have led him. If I speak with a

1 Shams al-Dīn al-Dhahabi, *Siyar Aʿlām al-Nubalāʾ*, Eleventh Edition, ed. Shuʿayb al-Arnaʾūṭ, Damascus: Muʾassasat al-Risālah, 1996, Vol.19, p.322.

2 Taj al-Dīn al-Subkī, *Ṭabaqāt al-Shāfiʿiyah al-Kubrā*, First Edition, ed. Muḥammad Maḥmūd al-Ṭannājī and ʿAbd al-Fattāḥ al-Ḥilw, Cairo: Fayṣal ʿĪsā al-Bābī al-Ḥalabī, 1964, Vol. 4, p. 101.

> philosopher, I shouldn't think of parting with him without setting about to ascertain the nature of his philosophy. Nor would I, if in the presence of a scholastic theologian, be content to quit his presence without first having probed his theology and the arguments on which he bases it. If I find myself with a mystic, I will probe the depths of his mystical awareness, and if a devout worshipper, scrutinize the basis for his intense devotion. I would not abandon the company of even a freethinker or atheist without seeking first to ascertain the causes that gave rise to his daring.[3]

This statement of al-Ghazālī's clearly evidences his passion for knowledge and his refusal to be cowed by the intellectual intimidation, arrogance and superiority so commonly found among extremists of every sect and religion.

In the preface to his book *al-Muṣṭaṣfā min ʿIlm al-Uṣūl (A Clarification of Legal Theory)*, Imām al-Ghazālī turned to the subject of reason and its value, saying, "Reason is the noblest of all things, being the vessel which conveys the message of religion and bears the sacred trust." Similarly, al-Ghazālī pointed out the importance of consistency between the content of sacred texts and the dictates of reason, both of which he viewed as being genuine sources of knowledge. He wrote,

> Reason cannot dispense with revelation, just as revelation cannot dispense with reason. Those who call for blind imitation while setting reason aside are ignorant, whereas those who content themselves with a mere reliance upon reason without the light provided by the Qurʾān and the Sunnah are arrogant and deluded. Beware lest you fall into either of these camps. Rather, draw upon both of these sources at once. The rational sciences might be likened to nutritious food, and the religious sciences to healing medicine.[4]

This was a response to certain people of Imām al-Ghazālī's generation who, upon receiving divine revelation, insisted on shunning reason.

---

3 Al-Ghazālī, *al-Munqidh min al-Ḍalāl*, First Edition, Sidon, Lebanon: al-Maktabah al-ʿAṣriyah, 2017, p. 88.

4 *Iḥyaʾ ʿUlūm al-Dīn*, Vol. 3, p. 17.

Such people would take a religious text out of its context, attempt to interpret it in an abstract manner, and then restore it to its original context. In so doing, they would disconnect the general meaning from the context, and there would be no agreement. Spiritual insight was nonexistent, physical sight absent, and understanding lost. On the same page, al-Ghazālī went on to say, "There are those who suppose that the rational sciences contradict the Islamic sciences, and that they could never be reconciled. Such a supposition arises from an inward blindness from which we beg God's protection." To this al-Ghazālī added, "In fact, those who hold to such a belief might well see some Islamic sciences as contradicting others such that they, too, could never be reconciled. On this basis they will suppose, further, that there is contradiction within the religion itself. Hence they will find themselves bewildered and confused, and slip out of the religion's grip as a thread slips out of a needle."

Imām al-Ghazālī warred fiercely against the practice of crippling people's minds in such a way that one authoritative religious text was seen to be pitted against another. There was something else, however, which he warred against with equal ferocity, namely, the bane of blind imitation that had afflicted the Islamic society of his day. People of al-Ghazālī's generation were embroiled in a tug-of-war among countless conflicting sectarian views and distracted by side issues that branched out every which way. The cacophonous details of these fruitless debates had plunged them into a quagmire of worn-out disputes and intellectual one-upmanship, and all for the sake of this or that innovative interpretation or point of view that had not been settled with definitive certainty. Imām al-Ghazālī's response to this state of affairs was to stress the importance of returning to an imitation of our Master the Messenger of God (may God grant him blessings and peace), the Imām and guide of the entire Muslim community who had mastered all knowledge and was fully versed in the wise purposes and aims of the Qur'ān and the Sunnah. Al-Ghazālī wrote,

> The Bringer of the Law of Islam, may God's blessings and peace be upon him, is to be imitated with respect to everything he commanded and said. As for the Companions, may God be pleased with them, they are only to be imitated insofar as what

> they did indicates that they had listened to the Messenger of God, may God bless him and grant him peace. Furthermore, when one of the Companions imitated the Bringer of the Law based on the acceptance of what he had said and done, the Companion was expected to be keen to understand the wisdom underlying the words and actions he was imitating. The imitator undertakes a given action because the Bringer of the Law, may God bless him and grant him peace, undertook the action before him. In addition, however, the imitator should search earnestly for the hidden wisdom underlying the actions and words he is imitating, for if he contents himself simply with memorizing what was said or done, he will be a vessel for knowledge, but not a true knower. Therefore, a person used to be referred to not as "a knower," but only as "a vessel of knowledge" if he simply memorized actions and words without familiarizing himself with their underlying wisdom and mysteries. Those who remove the veils from their hearts by the light of guidance will themselves be followed and imitated by others, as a result of which they should imitate no one.[5]

Imām al-Ghazālī warned his readers against falling under the control of imitators who parrot phrases from this or that scholar or this or that religious text without a proper understanding of the evidence for their views, and without an awareness of the ranks of Qurʾānic evidence and the gradation of texts, some of which provide more definitive proof than others, and some of which convey more definitive meanings than others. Such individuals' infatuation with controlling the discourse addressed to lay people has embroiled them in many a grave offense, particularly those of bigotry and rigidity. In this connection, al-Ghazālī declared,

> When someone follows a set of teachings he has heard in a spirit of blind imitation, he adheres to it rigidly and defends it in a fanatic, bigoted manner. He simply obeys what he has heard without having been convinced of its truth through insight and personal experience. Such a person becomes so bound by his belief that he is unable to go beyond it. At this point, no other

5 Ibid, Vol. 1, p. 78.

> belief would even be conceivable to him. His entire view of things is dependent on what he has heard and embraced as his belief. Hence, if a glimmer of light appeared in the distance such that he entertains, however briefly, some understanding of things that conflicts with what he has heard, the "demon of imitation" will take over. He might say to himself, "How could such a thing even occur to you? It goes against what your forefathers have always believed!" Concluding that this unaccustomed thought or idea is some devilish deceit, he spurns it and goes on the defensive against anything that might remotely resemble it. This is why the Sufis say that knowledge is a veil. By "knowledge" here, they are referring to the doctrines that most people cling to based on nothing but blind imitation, or based on contentious arguments framed by bigoted proponents of this sect or that and placed in their mouths.[6]

This is because an imitator is not a knower in the precise sense of the word, even if he has memorized the relevant texts and sayings and spouts them at the appropriate times. On the contrary, such a person prevents himself from being illumined with the radiance of knowledge. He is forever tied to Earth because he is too lazy to exert the diligent effort required to arrive at an understanding of his own. He imprisons himself within the confines of this or that opinion or school of thought, fleeing from the conceit of knowledge to the devil of blind imitation. Those who engage in the calamitous practice of imitation in the guise of knowledge portray knowledge as being limited to the understanding of this or that individual, or this or that group of ancient or modern thinkers, while claiming that truth, understanding and authority are the sole province of this individual or group. This is the essence of the fanaticism and partisanship that divide Muslims into sects and factions. Attitudes such as these have led some extremists to brand those who disagree with them as infidels. It should be borne in mind, moreover, that extremists who accuse other believers of being infidels do so not on the basis of people's stances on texts that are of definitive attestation and meaning (such as clearly understood passages of the Qurʾān) but,

---

6 Ibid., Vol. 1, p. 284.

rather, their stances on sectarian teachings that are only speculative in nature. It appears that the culture of extremism that manifests itself in today's *takfīrī* movement had begun spreading in al-Ghazālī's day as well. Wanting to combat this odious mindset, Imām al-Ghazālī wrote in his *al-Iqtiṣād fī al-Iʿtiqād (Moderation in Belief)*,

> Most of those who behave in this manner are animated by bigoted fanaticism, and by a belief that they have the duty to brand as an infidel anyone who disbelieves the Apostle. The people so branded are not actual disbelievers, however, nor is it clear to us that a mistaken interpretation requires that one be labeled an infidel. Rather, there has to be evidence to back up such a claim. It is a matter of definitive certainty that a kind of spiritual protection *(ʿiṣmah)* is conferred upon whoever has uttered the testimony of faith, that is, *lā ilāha illā God* ("There is no god but God"). Such protection can therefore only be reversed on the basis of something equally definitive. Those who go to excess in declaring others infidels do so not on the basis of some proof, since proof must be either founded upon a valid source, or upon an analogy drawn on the basis of such a source. The fundamental condition for declaring someone an infidel is an explicit statement of disbelief. Short of this, there is no basis for such a claim, and the person concerned will be included within the *ʿiṣmah*, or protected status, conferred upon those who have uttered the testimony of faith: *lā ilāha illā God.*[7]

As for philosophy, Imām al-Ghazālī plumbed its depths and involved himself fully in its controversies. This interest and concern on al-Ghazālī's part is evidenced by his well-known work *Tahafut al-Falasifah (The Incoherence of the Philosophers)*, to which Ibn Rushd (Averroes) penned a rebuttal in his *Tahafut al-Tahafut (Incoherence of the Incoherence)*. As I see it, however, al-Ghazālī's aim in this work was not to condemn philosophy as an independent discipline but, rather, to challenge the practice of mingling philosophy with religion as had been done by theologians of other religions in their attempts to know God Almighty and His attributes, to identify what

7 Al-Ghazālī, *al-Iqtiṣād fī al-Iʿtiqād*, First Edition, Beirut: Dār al-Kutub al-ʿIlmiyah, 2004, Vol. 1, p. 136.

things are possible or impossible for God, and the like. In al-Ghazālī's understanding, religion is what came directly on God's authority in the Qurʾān, and what has come down to us on the authority of the Messenger of God (may God's blessings and peace be upon him and his descendants) through the Sunnah. Imām al-Ghazālī's view was that by giving them the Qurʾān and the Sunnah of the Prophet, God Almighty has spared Muslims the need to formulate a philosophy in order to compensate for inadequacies in the books attributed to the prophets. All basic religious concepts, from the divine names and attributes to the fundamental truths, aims and wise purposes of the religion's doctrines and practices, are provided by the Qurʾān and the Sunnah, thereby eliminating the need for philosophy as a para-religious support system, as it were.

Similarly, al-Ghazālī came in for harsh criticism, especially among later scholars, for the weakly attested hadiths he cited in *The Revival of the Religious Sciences*. Perhaps al-Ghazālī had a particular line of thought which he felt required the citation of such hadiths in that context. Be that as it may, anyone who has familiarized himself with al-Ghazālī's other writings, including, for example, his valuable work *Taḥsīn al-Maʾākhidh fī ʿIlm al-Khilāf (Establishment of Sources for the Science of Proper Argumentation in Resolving Disagreements Among Islamic Scholars)* would be ashamed to describe Imām al-Ghazālī as having had a shallow knowledge of the hadith sciences.

Nor did Imām al-Ghazālī forget to direct criticism and blame at corrupt scholars who had sold their consciences to worldly powers from which they stood to gain wealth, position and influence. He made clear that tyrants make use of scholars in the hope of lending religious or philosophical legitimacy to their unjust practices. In this way, they seek to deter people from grumbling and rising up to change things for the better. Al-Ghazālī wrote,

> It was the wont of scholars of integrity to command what was good and forbid what was evil. Such scholars were indifferent to the power wielded by sultans and kings, since they relied on God Almighty to guard them, and on God's bounty to provide for their needs. They were content in the knowledge that God would grant them sustenance through their witness to His Oneness and Sovereignty. When their intention before God was

> pure and steadfast, their words were infused with power, and hardened hearts softened. Nowadays, by contrast, greed and ambition have tied scholars' tongues and caused them to fall silent. Even if they speak, their words do nothing to improve their situations, and they meet with no success. If they were sincere in seeking true knowledge, they would be successful. A corrupt citizenry is caused by corrupt rulers, corrupt rulers are caused by a corrupt intelligentsia, and the intelligentsia are corrupted when their hearts are taken over by the love of money and prestige. Those who have been possessed by love of the world will be unable to influence even the lowest of the low. How much less able will they be, then, to hold sway over the high and mighty? In either case, it is God whose aid must be sought.[8]

Imām al-Ghazālī himself used to send stern letters to monarchs and ministers, urging them to act justly and reminding them of their responsibilities before God Almighty and before the people they had been placed in power to serve. In all of this, the great Imām—God have mercy on his soul—might just as well have been addressing those in our own day and age. Indeed, this may have been a kind of saintly miracle on his part.

Imām al-Ghazālī was among the finest of jurists. Nevertheless, he avoided being prolix and detailed in his discussions lest he lose his lay audience in the minutiae of legal particulars. In the jurisprudence of Islamic rites of worship, for example, he viewed the ablution primarily as a means of washing the heart, and only secondarily as a means of washing the face and other parts of the body. Similarly, in the jurisprudence of commercial and governmental transactions, he held that if people have good intentions and restrain themselves from greed, they will profit in both a worldly and otherworldly sense. At the same time, however, he warned his readers not to forfeit the profit of the world to come for the sake of profit in the earthly realm.

Imām al-Ghazālī helped to lay the foundations for what has come to be termed "the jurisprudence of priorities." He stated,

> Disobedience is a visible phenomenon. What is not so visible is

---

8 *Iḥyāʾ ʿUlūm al-Dīn*, Vol. 1, p. 357.

> the act of placing higher priority on some acts of obedience than one does on others, such as when we place greater importance on obligatory acts of obedience than we do on voluntary ones, on individual acts of obedience than on acts of obedience required of the community as a whole, on communal acts of obedience that no one has yet carried out than on those that have already been carried out, on more important obligatory acts than on less important ones, and on actions whose validity depends on their being performed within a finite time period than on those not bound by such a time frame.[9]

In application of this principle, Imām al-Ghazālī issued a fatwa in which he gave preference to distributing alms to the poor and needy and to charitable enterprises with the money one would have spent to perform the Hajj to Mecca if one has already done so in the past and has, thereby, fulfilled one's religious obligation with respect to the Hajj. In illustration of this ruling he narrated a story about a particular pious ascetic. This is how the story goes:

> A man came to bid farewell to Bishr Bin al-Ḥārith al-Ḥāfī, saying, "I've decided to perform the Hajj. Do you have any instructions for me?"
>
> Bishr replied, "How much have you set aside for your expenses?"
>
> "Two thousand dirhams," said the man. Bishr then asked him, "What is it that you wish to achieve through this Hajj? Self-denial? To satisfy a longing to see the Holy Kaaba? To win God's approval?"
>
> "To win God's approval," the man replied. "So, then," Bishr asked the man, "If you could be certain of winning God's approval by spending two thousand dinars while remaining at home, would you do it?"
>
> "Yes, I would," replied the man.
>
> "All right then," Bishr told him, "go and give it to ten souls: to someone in debt to repay what he owes, to a poor person to buy new clothes, to a breadwinner so as to enrich his dependents, to an orphan's caregiver so as give joy to his

9 Ibid., Vol. 3, p. 403.

> heart. And if your heart is strong enough to do so, give it all to one person. To bring joy to a Muslim's heart, bring aid to the distressed, remove harm and strengthen the weak is better than a hundred pilgrimages once one has performed the single obligatory pilgrimage required of every Muslim. So, then, rise and distribute this aid as we have instructed you. Otherwise, tell us what you would prefer."
>
> "O Abū Naṣr," the man replied, "the journey in my heart is the most powerful."
>
> Upon hearing this, Bishr smiled, may God have mercy on him, and, coming up to the man, said, "If wealth is amassed through dishonest commerce and unsavory dealings, you will be prompted to fulfill some selfish desire therewith, and to display your righteous actions before others rather than concealing them to ensure that your reward is from God alone. God has pledged to accept no action unless it is prompted by true piety and fear of Him."[10]

Al-Ghazālī also exposed the miserly rich who cling to money out of avarice, and then busy themselves with physical acts of worship such as fasting, spending the night in prayer, and reading the Qurʾān from beginning to end. He described them as "conceited and self-deceived." Their sight veiled by self-love, such people fail to realize that true wealth consists of reliance on and faith in God Almighty and putting others before oneself. Such people have not seen that the truly rich individual is not the one who possesses everything, but the one who needs nothing. Imām al-Ghazālī instructed his listeners and readers to refrain from performing supererogatory pilgrimages to Mecca if the person governing Mecca was burdening pilgrims with excessive taxation or was imposing excessive fees on the major and minor pilgrimages (the Hajj and the ʿUmrah respectively). In such situations, stated al-Ghazālī, performance of the pilgrimage becomes a way of aiding and abetting unjust rulers, submitting unduly to their tyranny, and placing Muslims in a humiliating position as though they were paying a *jizyah*.

Yet despite his abundant wisdom, al-Ghazālī insisted that he

---

10 Ibid., Vol. 3, p. 498.

needed to learn more himself before he preached to others. In his *Ṭabaqāt al-Shāfiʿiyyah al-Kubrā*, al-Subkī wrote, "He [al-Ghazālī] was once asked why he rarely preached, to which he replied, 'I do not see myself as worthy of preaching. Preaching is a kind of *zakah* which, in order to be qualified to distribute it, one must first have a sufficient store of lessons taken to heart. Only those who have accumulated this minimum store are entitled to distribute such *zakah*.'"[11]

As we journey with Imām al-Ghazālī through his *The Revival of the Sciences of Religion*, we encounter a jurisprudence whose words pulsate with life, a religion that is an integral whole, and a religious perspective that is reformist and comprehensive. Beginning with correct doctrine, al-Ghazālī sets out with us on a trek that combines jurisprudence with inner purification. At some point along the way, however, jurisprudence reaches its limit and falls away. Then nothing remains but spiritual purification, charity, and love, which continue to escort us on our way to communion with God Almighty. Throughout this process, never does al-Ghazālī tear down or destroy; he only builds up and strengthens. Never once does he alienate or separate; he only joins and unites. After all, never has there been any conflict between doctrine, jurisprudence, and self-purification.

Imām al-Ghazālī has been loved dearly by scholars of true beneficence, self-purification, the subtle graces and mystical union, who give him a place of prominence in these disciplines. He is likewise revered among scholars of the fundamentals of jurisprudence, who accord him the highest of ranks in this lofty and exacting science. He is venerated by jurists with expertise in questions of subtle distinctions for his well-merited and, indeed, incomparable place of standing in the Shāfiʿī school of jurisprudence. Similarly, as a keen-eyed scholastic well-versed in the intricacies of the sciences of theoretical monotheism, in the context of which he authored many an original interpretation within the Ashʿarī school, he has long been a well-trusted source among scholars of the principles of the religion. To this day, al-Ghazālī's works guide students of philosophy and logic, who glean from his aphorisms and his arguments alike a refined Islamic philosophy steeped in the nectar of divine knowledge

---

11 Al-Subkī, *Ṭabaqāt al-Shāfiʿiyah al-Kubrā*, op. cit., Vol. 4, p. 122.

and loving communion. And last but not least, Imām al-Ghazālī has been cherished for his love of God Almighty, God's messengers, God's religion and God's revealed messages, his unstinting devotion in the service of them all, and his rare enthusiasm in the defense of the religious and humanitarian ethic that arises out of faith in the one most merciful, loving and bounteous Creator.

Imām al-Ghazālī devoted a good deal of thought to the beauty of the environment and human beings' duty toward their surroundings. In the chapter on actions to be avoided in the streets and thoroughfares, he listed leaving loads of food and grains lest they block the path, tying one's riding animal, throwing refuse, butchering animals, and disposing of household waste water.

A tour through Imām al-Ghazālī's gardens of spiritual delights is a luxuriant, rich, and varied excursion. May God have mercy on him and reward him most richly for the service he performed for Islam and the Muslim community down the ages. How profoundly we need the refined moderation he bequeathed to us in its most comprehensive expressions.

Praise be to God, Lord of the worlds.

Penned with praise, prayer, and surrender by
Shaykh Muhammad Bin Yahya al-Ninowy
Atlanta, Georgia
1 Rabīʿ al-Awwal of the year 1440 following the blessed migration of our Master, the Messenger of God, may God Almighty bless and grant peace to him and his descendants.
10 November, 2018

My dear sister and fine translator Nancy Roberts did a wonderful job translating this piece about Imām al-Ghazālī. She is gifted and blessed to have captured more than just the words I wrote about this great figure.

بسم الله الرحمن الرحيم

Translator's Introduction

> To me, it seems typical of Ghazālī's way of thought that the center of the book, the twentieth chapter, is devoted to the central figure in Islam, the Prophet Muḥammad.
>
> Annemarie Schimmel

In the course of translating this succinct treatise, it occurred to me that it reads very much as an accessible thematic synopsis of salient aspects of the ethico-moral character of the Noble Prophet—God bless him and grant him peace. In the 13 sections of this treatise or book, Imām al-Ghazālī provides brief descriptions and accounts of his physical deportment, manners and habits, family life at home and community life with his Companions, interactions with friends and enemies, along with his bravery, generosity, sense of humor, forgiving nature and miracles. For readers who are looking for a short, direct biographical introduction to the "Ethics of Prophethood" without navigating through the sometimes dense and lengthy socio-historical backdrop given in larger biographical works, this little book of al-Ghazālī will be most welcome.

Such indeed appears to be the express intention of Ghazālī when he composed Book XX of his *magnum opus*, *Iḥyāʾ ʿUlūm al-Dīn*, as the concluding chapter 10 of the "Norms of Daily Life," which constitutes the second of the four Quarters of the *Iḥyāʾ*. He says in his introduction:

> I have deemed it proper to confine myself in this book to recounting [various aspects of] the moral comportment of the Messenger of God—God bless him and grant him peace.... without mentioning their chains of attested authorities, in order that there be gathered in this book—together with

> assembling the manners of ethical conduct—the renewal of belief and its reinforcement by way of bearing witness to his noble etiquettes, each of which bears witness with utmost certitude that he is the noblest of the creation of God Most High, the most elevated in rank and the most magnificent in stature, and hence, how much more so the truth of this fact when all his etiquettes are brought together and integrated.[1]

Hence, he intends to recapitulate indirectly all the religiously approved norms of daily life upon which he has expounded in the previous nine books in this last volume on the comprehensive decorum of the Noble Prophet—God bless him and grant him peace. This *adāb* is to be understood as the supreme pattern in the light of which people may scrutinize their daily habits and evaluate for themselves the extent to which they realize or frustrate those religious norms.

The importance of the Noble Prophet's *sīrah* or biography for Muslims in their endeavor to realize Islam as the *true* Religion—especially in this postmodernist age of the "deconsecration of values"[2]—is borne out by Professor al-Attas's pertinent observation, which I would like to cite at some length here:

> Religion consists not only of the affirmation of the Unity of God (*al-tawḥīd*), but also of the *manner* and *form* in which we verify that affirmation as shown by His last Prophet, who confirmed, perfected and consolidated the manner and form of affirmation and verification of prophets before him. This manner and form of verification is the manner and form of submission to God. The test of *true affirmation* of the Unity of God, then, is the *form of submission* to that God.[3] It is only because the form of submission enacted by the religion that affirms the Unity of God is *true to the verification of such*

---

1 *Iḥyā᾽ ʿUlūm al-Dīn*, 10 vols. (Jeddah: Dār al-Minhāj, 2011), 4:709-710.

2 Literally to desecrate or disassociate values or things from any notions of the sacred, divine or transcendent, and of final and ultimate purpose; the term refers to the "rendering transient and relative all cultural creations and every value system," including "religion and worldviews having ultimate and final significance." For further elaboration, see Syed Muhammad Naqib al-Attas, *Islam and Secularism*, 2nd impression (Kuala Lumpur: ISTAC, 1993), 18-19.

3 *Prolegomena to the Metaphysics of Islam: An Exposition of the Fundamental Elements of the Worldview of Islam* (Kuala Lumpur: ISTAC, 2001), 11 (italics original).

> *affirmation* that that particular religion is called Islam. Islam, then, is not merely a verbal noun signifying submission; it is also *the name of a particular religion* descriptive of true submission, as well as the *definition of religion*: submission to God.

In short, the Prophet—God bless him and grant him peace—has already shown people in his very person, words and deeds the clear path to (and hence the *form of*) true submission to our Creator and Sustainer, and thus, they need to conscientiously emulate him if they are really serious about submitting themselves to Him. Therefore,

> He is the perfect model for every Muslim male and female; adolescent, middle-aged and old, in such wise that Muslims do not suffer from the crises of identity. Because of him the external structure or pattern of Muslim society is not divided by the gap of generations such as we find prevalent in Western society.[4]

This translation, and the footnote references to ḥadīths and other texts therein, are based for the most part on the Dār al-Minhāj edition of the *Iḥyāʾ*,[5] with occasional collating with the Dār al-Fayḥāʾ edition[6] and with the *Itḥāf*,[7] especially to clarify ambiguous phrases and expressions, and to cross-refer documentations of ḥadīths, most of which are related by al-Bukhārī, Muslim, al-Tirmidhī, Ibn Mājah, Abū Dāwūd and al-Nasāʾī. Serious students of ḥadīths and *āthār* are however well-advised to refer directly to their original Arabic sources and al-ʿIrāqī's documentation (*takhrīj*) in his *Mughnī*,[8] or collate with alternative editions of the relevant ḥadīth collections. I have also made use of an earlier published translation by Leon Zolondek[9] (made accessible to me by Muhammad Hozien), especially to discern some of the translational strategies he used to render some

---

4 *Prolegomena*, 80-81.

5 10 vols. (Jeddah: Dār al-Minhāj, 2011).

6 Edited by ʿAlī Muḥammad Muṣṭafā and Saʿīd al-Maḥāsinī, 6 vols. (Damascus: Dār al-Fayḥāʾ, 2010).

7 Murtaḍā al-Zābidī, *Itḥāf Ṣādat al-Muttaqīn bi Sharḥ Iḥyāʾ ʿUlūm al-Dīn* (Beirut: Dār Iḥyāʾ al-Turāth al-ʿArabī, 1994).

8 Zayn al-Dīn Abū Faḍl ʿAbd al-Raḥīm ibn al-Ḥusayn al-ʿIrāqī (d. 806 AH), *al-Mughnī ʿan al-Asfār fī al-Asfār fī Takhrīj mā fī al-Iḥyāʾ min al-Akhbār* (Cairo: Dar al-Hadith, 1992).

9 Leon Zolondek, *Book XX of al-Ghazālī's Iḥyāʾ ʿUlūm al-Dīn* (Leiden: Brill, 1963).

tricky passages readable as well as understandable. On the whole, the footnoting has been deliberately kept to a bare minimum with very little attempt to provide some larger socio-historical context, for which the reader can refer to the larger more detailed works of *sīrah*, such as al-Būṭī's authoritative *Fiqh al-Sīrah*.[10] My translations of verses of the Qur'ān are largely based on, and adaptations of, Pickthall's[11] and Cleary's.[12]

I wish to express my gratitude to my dear friend, Isa Robert Martin, a scholar and teacher of English, for finding time to go through my translation thus making it less awkward and more readable; to an accomplished, professional Arabic-English translator and scholar of Islamic religious sciences (who does not wish to be named) for helping to ensure the translation's linguistic felicity and semantic fidelity to the original text; to Professor David Burrell for applying his keen and experienced editorial eye over the final draft; to Shaykh Walead Mosaad for his Preface; to Dr. Afifi al-Akiti for penning his learned and thoughtful Foreword; and to Shaykh Ninowy for his beautiful Introduction. My thanks are also due to Dr. Talal Azem and Sidi Yusuf Jha for their critical perusal of the final draft. Whatever flaws that remain must of course be attributed only to my translational defects and inadequacies.

I most surely owe a huge debt of gratitude to Virginia Gray Henry and Sidi Muhammad Hozien of Fons Vitae for so kindly proposing to me the undertaking of this translation project way

---

10 Trans. Nancy Roberts as *Jurisprudence of the Prophetic Biography and a Brief History of the Rightly-Guided Caliphate*, 5th ed. (Damascus: Dar al-Fikr, 2010); see also Muḥammad Ḥamīdullāh, *Le Prophete del' Islam: Sa Vie et Son Ouevre*, trans. Mahmood Ahmad Ghazi, *The Life and Work of the Prophet of Islam* (Islamabad: Islamic Research Institute, 1998). Notable classical biographical works focusing (like Ghazālī's) on Prophetic decorum is al-Qāḍī Iyāḍ ibn Mūsā al-Yahsūbī, *al-Shifāʾ bi Ḥuqūq al-Muṣṭafā* (*The Healing by Observing the Rights of the Chosen Prophet*), trans. Aisha Abdarrahman Bewley as *Muhammad, Messenger of Allah: Ash-Shifa of Qadi ʿIyad*, rev ed. (Norwich: Diwan Press, 2011), and Muḥammad ibn Īsā al-Tirmidhī, *al-Shamāʾil al-Muḥammadiyyah* (*The Muḥammadan Perfections*), trans. Bahaa Addin Ibrahim Ahmed Shalaby, *The Characteristics of Prophet Muhammed*, ed. Selma Cook (Al-Manṣūrah: Dār al-Manārah, 2003); cf. idem, Muhtar Holland, trans., *A Potrait of the Prophet as Seen by His Contemporaries* (Fons Vitae, 2014).

11 Muhammad Marmaduke Pickthall, *The Glorious Qurʾān: Text and Explanatory Translation* (Mecca: Muslim World League, 1977).

12 Thomas Cleary, *The Qurʾan: A New Translation* (Starlatch, 2004).

back in 2013 (how time flies!), and for thereafter graciously bearing with my tardiness in getting it completed. But as the saying goes, "*kullu ātin qarīb*," (all that arrives is near), so all is well that ends well! Neville Blakmore, Jr. and Nancy Roberts, also of Fons Vitae, deserve mention too for so diligently making the publication process as smooth as possible for all concerned.

Another thing that crossed my mind in the course of seeing this project to satisfying fruition is that translation is one thing, but *emulation* quite another. Emulation, in this regard, is a much more challenging art of translation. May God increase me and readers in the conscientious emulation of His noble Prophet—blessing and peace be upon him—and thereby render this work as a noble witness *for* us in the eternal vastness of the Afterlife, *āmīn yā Rabb al-ʿālamīn!*

ʿAdī Setia
Dusun Padi
Terengganu, Malaysia
11 Ramadan 1439
27 May 2018

Dedicated to
Professor Syed Muhammad Naquib al-Attas
and the Worldview of Islam

THE BOOK OF PROPHETIC ETHICS AND THE COURTESIES OF LIVING

Author's Introduction

In the Name of God, Most Merciful, Most Compassionate

All praise be to God, Who has created everything and then perfected its creation and proportion; Who has refined His Prophet, Muḥammad—God bless him and grant him peace—and then perfected his refinement, and purified his character and morals; then took him as His chosen and beloved, and facilitated his imitation for whomever He has willed to cleanse and barred from acquiring his morals whomever He has willed to debase. May God bless Muḥammad, chief of the Messengers, and his good and pure family, and grant them peace in abundance.

And now to proceed. Indeed, our external deportment is but an indicator of our internal comportment, and the activities of our limbs are but the fruits of our thoughts; for deeds are but the consequence of inner character, and ethical conduct the distillate of knowledge, while the inner secrets of the hearts are but the roots of actions and their wellsprings. The lights from these inner secrets shine upon the bodily externalities, thereby adorning and embellishing them, and replacing with refined features their abhorrent and wicked ones. Hence, those whose hearts are not devoted in humility, their limbs are likewise not devoted in humbleness; and those whose chests are not repositories of divine lights, their external conduct will not be enfolded in the splendor of Prophetic decorum.

Verily, I have resolved to bring to conclusion the "Quarter on the Norms of Daily Life" of this Book[1] with a book[2] that deals comprehensively with the "Comportment of Living" in order that it would not be difficult for students to extract it from the entirety of the books.[3] But then I noticed that each book of the "Quarter of Devotions" and the "Quarter of the Norms of Daily Life" has already come with a discussion on some aspects of ethical comportment, and I am weary of repeating them and returning to them, for indeed, repetition is intolerable, and people's souls have a propensity to be inimical towards repetitions.

Therefore, I have deemed it proper to confine myself in this book to recounting the moral comportment of the Messenger of God—God bless him and grant him peace—and his ethical manners that have been transmitted of him through attested authority.[4] In this regard, I recount them together section by section without mentioning their chains of attested authorities, in order that there be gathered in this book—together with assembling the manners of ethical conduct—the renewal of belief and its reinforcement by way of bearing witness to his noble etiquettes. Each bears witness with utmost certitude that he is the noblest of the creation of God Most High, the most elevated in rank, and the most magnificent in stature, and hence, how much more so the truth of this fact when all his etiquettes are brought together and integrated.

Then I append to the recounting of his ethical comportment the mention of his physical deportment, followed by the mention of his miracles that have been validated in the reports, in order that they may clearly make known the nobilities of ethical comportment and disposition and remove the plug of deafness from the ears of the deniers of his Prophethood. God Most High is the Lord of facilitation towards the emulation of the Chief of the Messengers in regard to ethical comportment and moral conduct, as well as all

---

1 i.e., the *Iḥyāʾ* as a whole.

2 i.e., a chapter.

3 i.e., from the whole of the *Iḥyāʾ*, which comprises forty books or chapters; or, as most likely in the immediate context of the passage, from the whole of the 1st and 2nd Quarters, which together comprises 20 books.

4 i.e., reports (*ḥadīth* and *khabar*) with authenticated chains of transmission (*sanad*).

the other guideposts of the Religion, for He is indeed the One Who points the way for the perplexed and responds to the supplication of those in need.

We shall first of all give an account of his refinement by God Most High with the Qurʾān, then an account of the summaries of the refinements of his ethical comportment, then an account of a compilation of his manners and etiquettes, then an account of his speech and his sense of humor, then an account of his etiquettes and manners in the partaking of food, then an account of his etiquettes and manners of his attire, then an account of his forgiving nature despite his ability to censure, then an account of his turning away from whatever he disliked, then an account of his generosity and munificence, then an account of his courage and valor, then an account of his humility, then an account of his appearance and physical deportment, and then an account of the totality of his miracles and the signs of his veracity—God bless him and grant him peace.

1

An Account of the Refinement by God Most High of His Beloved and Chosen, Muḥammad (God Bless Him and Grant Him Peace)

THE Messenger of God—God bless him and grant him peace—was very imploring and supplicatory, perpetually beseeching God Most High to beautify him with the refinements of ethical comportment and the nobilities of character, for he used to say in his supplication, "O God, beautify my physical form and my ethical character."[1] And he would say, "O God, make me shun wicked character traits."[2] And so God Most High responded to his supplication in realization of His statement—glorified and exalted be He—"*Call upon Me and I will respond to you*."[3] He revealed to him the Qurʾān and refined him with it, and thus his ethical character was the Qurʾān.

Saʿd ibn Hishām said, "I visited ʿĀʾishah—God be well-pleased with her and her father—and I queried her regarding the ethical character of God's Messenger—God bless him and grant him peace—whereupon she said, 'Do you not read the Qurʾān?' I said, 'Indeed I do.' She said, 'The ethical character of God's Messenger— God bless

1 Narrated by Aḥmad in *al-Musnad* (1:403) and (6:68), of the ḥadīth of ʿAbdullāh ibn Masʿūd and ʿĀʾishah—God be pleased with them both; and Ibn Ḥibbān in his *Ṣaḥīḥ* (no. 959) of the ḥadīth of Ibn Masʿūd.

2 Narrated by al-Tirmidhī (no. 3591).

3 *al-Muʾmin* (The Believer), 40:60.

him and grant him peace—is the Qurʾān.'"[4]

The Qurʾān has indeed refined him by such statements of God Most High as, "*Take the course of forgiveness and command what is righteous, and turn away from the ignorant ones.*"[5]

And His statement, "*Verily God commands justice and magnanimity, and giving to the near of kin, and He forbids immorality, wickedness and infringement.*"[6]

And His statement—exalted be He, "*And show forebearance over what befalls you, for, verily, that is of the most resolute recourse in resolving affairs.*"[7]

And His statement, "*And indeed whosoever shows patience and forgives, that is surely of the most resolute recourse in resolving affairs.*"[8]

And His statement, "*So, forgive them and overlook them; verily God loves the magnanimous.*"[9]

And His statement, "*And let them excuse and pardon; do you not desire that God forgive you?*"[10]

And His statement, "*Fend off with what is better, for thereupon the one between you and whom there was enmity becomes as a bosom friend.*"[11]

And His statement, "*And those who control their anger and forgive people—and God loves the magnanimous.*"[12]

And His statement, "*Avoid much of suspicion, for indeed, some suspicion is a sin; and do not spy and do not let it be that some of you backbite another.*"[13]

When his two teeth were broken and he was wounded in the battle of Uḥud, and the blood began flowing down his face, he wiped it off while saying, "How shall a people be successful who stain the face of their Prophet with blood even as he calls them to their Lord?"

---

4 Narrated by Muslim (no. 746).

5 *al-Aʿrāf* (The Heights), 7:199.

6 *al-Naḥl* (The Bee), 16:90.

7 *Luqmān*, 31:17.

8 *al-Shūrā* (Counsel), 42:43.

9 *al-Māʾidah* (The Table-Spread), 5:13.

10 *al-Nūr* (Light), 24:22.

11 *Fuṣṣilat* (*Ḥā Mīm al-Sajdah*) (They Are Expounded), 41:34.

12 *Āl ʿImrān* (Family of ʿImrān), 3:134.

13 *al-Ḥujurāt* (The Private Apartments), 49:12.

Whereupon God Most High revealed (the verse), "*You have no say whatsoever in the matter*,"[14] as a refinement of him regarding the situation. The examples of these incidents in the Qurʾān in which he is refined are innumerable.

And he—God bless him and grant him peace—is the foremost person intended for refinement and improvement, and thereafter his light shone over the whole of creation; for he was refined by the Qurʾān and in turn the creation[15] was refined by him; and for that reason he—God bless him and grant him peace—said, "I have been sent to perfect the nobilities of ethical character."[16] Thereupon humankind was made desirous of good ethical character as we have expounded in the "Book of Training the Self and Refinement of Character,"[17] and so I shall not repeat it here.

Thereafter, when God Most High had perfected his character, He praised him for it, and thus He the Exalted declares, "*And indeed, you are most surely upon a magnificent character*."[18] And thus God, Glorified be He, how great indeed is His affair, and how consummate His munificence! Look at the comprehensiveness of His favor, how He bestows and thereupon praises; for He is the One Who adorned him with a noble character, and then He attributed it to him by saying, "*And indeed, you are most surely upon a magnificent character*."[19] Then, he—God bless him and grant him peace—makes it clear to humankind that God loves the nobilities of ethical character and detests lowliness of character.[20]

ʿAlī—God be well-pleased with him—said, "How wondrous is the Muslim man! His Muslim brother visits him with a need but he does not consider himself worthy of bestowing kindness; for even if he does not hope for recompense or harbor fear of punishment,

---

14 *Āl ʿImrān* (Family of ʿImrān), 3:128; narrated by Muslim (no. 1791), of the ḥadīth of Anas—God be pleased with him.

15 or humankind.

16 Related by Aḥmad in his *Musnad* (2:381), al-Bukhārī in *al-Adab al-Mufrad* (no. 273) and al-Bayhaqī in *al-Sunan al-Kubrā* (10:191).

17 Book 22 of the *Iḥyāʾ*.

18 *al-Qalam* (The Pen), 68:4.

19 *al-Qalam* (The Pen), 68:4.

20 Narrated by al-Ḥākim in *al-Mustadrak* (1:48) of the ḥadīth of Ṭalḥah ibn ʿUbaydullāh ibn Kirīz, al-Bayhaqī in *al-Sunan al-Kubrā* (10:191), and Hannād in *al-Zuhd* (no. 828).

it surely would behoove him to hasten toward the cultivation of the nobilities of ethical character, for it is among those things that point to the path of salvation."[21]

Whereupon a man said to ʿAlī, "Did you hear of this from God's Messenger—God bless him and grant him peace?"

He said, "Yes, and what is better than it? When the captives of (the clan of) Ṭayyiʾ were brought forth, a female captive[22] stood up amidst them and said, 'O, Muḥammad, would you consider that you set me free so that I am not rejoiced over because of my misfortune by the tribes of the Arabs? For verily, I am the daughter of the chief of my people, and my father used to safeguard his cherished possessions, give comfort to the troubled, sate the hungry, provide food, spread greetings of peace, and never once refused anyone seeking him in need. I am the daughter of Ḥātim al-Ṭayyiʾi.'

Whereupon he—God bless him and grant him peace—replied to her, 'O, female captive; this is truly the depiction of the believers. If your father had been Muslim we would have prayed for God's mercy on him. Let you free her, for her father used to love the nobilities of ethical character, and God verily loves the nobilities of character.' Then Abū Burdah bin Nayyār stood up and said, 'O Messenger of God! God loves the nobilities of ethical character?' He responded, 'By the One in Whose grip is my soul, none enters the Garden but those of good character.'"[23]

And it was related on the authority of Muʿādh ibn Jabal—God be well-pleased with him—from the Prophet—God bless him and grant him peace—that he said, "Verily God has enfolded Islām with the nobilities of ethical character and the refinements of good works. Among these are good social relationships, noble deeds, pleasant companionship, promoting righteousness, provisioning of food, spreading greetings of peace, visiting sick Muslims be they virtuous or iniquitous, escorting the funeral bier of a Muslim, pleasant converse with those you converse with be they Muslims or

---

21 This means that one should always show kindness in this situation, at least as an expression of personal virtue, even if recompense in the Afterlife for doing so is not taken into consideration.

22 She was Sufānah bint Ḥātim.

23 Narrated by al-Ḥakīm al-Tirmidhī in *Nawādir al-Uṣūl* (p. 229), al-Bayhaqī in *Dalāʾil al-Nubuwwah* (5:241), Ibn ʿAsākir in *Tārīkh Dimashq* (11:358).

disbelievers, showing reverence to Muslims of old age, answering invitations to food and inviting others to it, showing forgiveness, restoring good relations among people, generosity, munificence, big-heartedness, initiating greetings of peace, suppression of anger, forgiving of people; and keeping away from what Islam prohibits of frivolity, falsity, singing, all stringed musical instruments, seeking vengeance, hostility, lying, backbiting, stingyness, avarice, harshness, deception, cheating, calumny, bad companionship,[24] sundering of kinship, bad manners, arrogance, pride, vanity, overbearingness, haughtiness, indecency, obscenity, malice, envy, inconstancy,[25] infringement, aggression and oppression."[26]

Anas—God be well-pleased with him—said, "He did not leave aside a good counsel or a fine disposition except that he would call us toward it and command us to realize it; and he did not leave aside a deception (or a defect)[27] nor a disgrace except that he would warn us of it and forbid us from it; and all that is sufficed by this verse, "*Verily God commands justice and magnanimity, and giving to near of kin, and forbids immorality and iniquity*."[28]

And Muʿādh—God be well-pleased with him said, "God's Messenger—God bless him and grant him peace—has enjoined upon me, saying, 'O Muʿādh! I enjoin upon you to be mindful of God, to be truthful in speech, to fulfill agreements, to honor trusts, to eschew betrayal of trusts, to care for the neighbor, to show kindness to orphans, to be soft-spoken, to spread greetings of peace, to do good work, to shorten expectations, to be constant in faith, to acquire understanding of the Qurʾān, to desire the Afterlife, to be concerned about the Reckoning, and to be humble. And I forbid you to disparage the sagacious, or to give lie to the truthful, or to obey the sinful, or to disobey a just ruler, or to sow corruption in

---

24 or sowing discord in relationship between friends or relatives.

25 or frivolity and flippancy.

26 al-Ḥāfiẓ al-ʿIrāqī says that he is not aware of this long ḥadīth; but see the similar ḥadīth of Muʿādh after the next ḥadīth

27 Translating for "...or he said, 'a defect'....".

28 *al-Naḥl* (The Bee),16:90; al-Ḥāfiẓ al-ʿIrāqī says he is not aware of the chain (*sanad*) for this ḥadīth, but that it is sound from the viewpoint of its actuality (or meaning, *al-wāqiʿ*); al-Ṭabarānī has related a ḥadīth of similar meaning in *al-Kabīr* (9:132), of the ḥadīth of Ibn Masʿūd—God be well-pleased with him.

the earth. And I enjoin upon you to be mindful of God at every tree, rock, and settlement, and that you exhibit repentance for every sin—secretly for hidden sins, and publicly for open sins.'"[29]

This, then, is the manner in which he has disciplined the bondservants of God, and called them toward the nobilities of ethical character and refinements of virtuous conduct.[30]

29 Related by Abū Nuʿaym in *al-Ḥilyah* (1:240), al-Bayhaqī in *al-Zuhd al-Kabīr* (no. 956), and al-Khaṭīb al-Baghdādī in *Tārīkh Baghdād* (8:434).

30 For more elaboration on the ethical and moral discipline of God's Messenger—God bless him and grant him peace—please see al-Laḥjī, *Muntahā al-Sūl* (2:316-385).

2

An Account of a Portion of His Nobilities of Ethical Character (God Bless Him and Grant Him Peace) That Have Been Brought Together by Some of the Scholars and Assembled from the Reports

THEY said: The Prophet—God bless him and grant him peace—was the most forebearing,[1] courageous,[2] just,[3] and chaste of people. His hand never once touched the hand of a woman over whom he had no ownership, or with whom he had no bond of marriage, or who was not an unmarriageable kin for him to marry.[4]

And he was the most generous of people, for not a dinar[5] or dirham[6] would be in his possession when he retired in the evening. If some money remained and he could not find anyone to give it to even when evening had come upon him, he would not return to

---

1 or gentle; as related in the book by Abū al-Shaykh, *Akhlāq al-Nabiyy wa Ādābihi* (no. 173) of the ḥadīth of ʿAbd al-Raḥmān ibn Abzā—God be pleased with him; and in *Ṣaḥīḥ ibn Ḥibbān* (no. 288) of the ḥadīth of ʿAbdullāh ibn Salām—God be pleased with him.

2 As related in *Ṣaḥīḥ al-Bukhārī* (no. 2820) and *Ṣaḥīḥ Muslim* (no. 2307).

3 As related in the *Shamāʾil* of al-Tirmidhī (no. 336) of the ḥadīth of Sayyidinā ʿAlī—God ennoble his countenance.

4 As related in *Ṣaḥīḥ al-Bukhārī* (no. 2713) and *Ṣaḥīḥ Muslim* (no. 1866) of the ḥadīth of ʿĀʾishah—God be pleased with her; and in al-Tirmidhī (no. 3306) on the authority of Ṭāwūs.

5 a gold coin or gold piece of about 4.25 grams of pure gold.

6 a silver coin or silver piece of about 3.975 grams of pure silver.

his dwelling until he had given it away to someone in need of it.[7]

And from what God had bestowed upon him he would only take a year's supply of food for himself, and it would be what was most readily available, such as dates and barley, while the rest of it he gave away to be spent in the path of God.[8]

He would not be asked for something except that he would give it,[9] and so he would go back and take it from his yearly provision giving preference to the one asking over himself, such that it would often be the case that he found himself in need before the year was out, should nothing else come his way.[10]

And he used to mend his sandals, patch his garment, assist with the household chores,[11] and cut up the meat with his womenfolk.[12] He was the most bashful of people, so much so that he would not fix his gaze on the face of anyone.[13]

He answered the invitations of both slaves and free-men,[14] accepted gifts even if it were only a draught of milk or a leg of rabbit meat, and he would requite in kind.[15] He would eat this[16] but he would not eat what was given out in charity. He was not aloof in responding to either the bondswomen or the poor.

He would get angry for the sake of his Lord—glorified and

---

7 Related by Abū Dāwūd (no. 3055) and Ibn Ḥibbān in his *Ṣaḥīḥ* (no. 6351) of the ḥadīth of Bilāl—God be pleased with him.

8 i.e., for some charitable cause.

9 As related in *Ṣaḥīḥ al-Bukhārī* (nos. 1277, 2093) of the ḥadīth of Sahl ibn Saʿd—God be pleased with him, and in *Ṣaḥīḥ Muslim* (no. 2312) of the ḥadīth of Anas—God be pleased with him.

10 As related in *Ṣaḥīḥ al-Bukhari* (no. 2916) of the ḥadīth of ʿĀʾishah—God be pleased with her.

11 As related by Aḥmad in *al-Musnad* (6:167) of the ḥadīth of ʿĀʾishah—God be pleased with her.

12 As related by Aḥmad in *al-Musnad* (6:94) of the ḥadīth of ʿĀʾishah—God be pleased with her.

13 As related in *Ṣaḥīḥ al-Bukhari* (no. 3562) and *Sahih* Muslim (no. 2320) of the ḥadīth of Abū Saʿīd al-Khudrī— God be pleased with him; and see also the *Jawāmiʿ al-Sīrah* of Ibn Ḥazm (p. 33).

14 As related by al-Tirmidhī (no. 1017), and Ibn Mājah (no. 4178) of the ḥadīth of Anas—God be pleased with him.

15 As related by al-Bukhārī (nos. 1662, 2572, 2585) of the ḥadīth of ʿĀʾishah and others—God be pleased with them; and Muslim (nos. 1123, 1953).

16 i.e., what was gifted to him as a present.

exalted be He—but he would not be angry for his own sake;[17] and he would honor what was right even if it might bring about some disadvantage upon himself or his Companions.[18]

He was offered the assistance of some polytheists in his struggle against other polytheists when he was few in number and in need of augmenting the number of those who were already with him even if by only a single man, but he refused and said, "We most certainly do not seek to attain to victory with the assistance of polytheists."[19]

One of the best and most virtuous of his Companions was found murdered amongst the Jews but he did not deal unjustly with them nor did he go beyond what was stringently upright. Instead, he paid the blood money of a hundred she-camels for him even though his Companions could not spare even a single camel with which they could fortify themselves.[20]

Sometimes he would fasten a stone to his stomach in order to assuage his hunger,[21] and sometimes he would eat whatever was at hand without refusing what he found available and without being fastidious about food that was permissible.[22] If he found some dried dates without bread he ate them.[23] If he found some broiled meat he ate it.[24] If he found some bread, whether barley or wheat he ate it.[25] If there were some sweet-dish or honey he ate it.[26] If there were

---

17 As related by al-Bukharī (no. 3560) and Muslim (no. 2327) of the ḥadīth of ʿĀʾishah; and by al-Tirmidhī in *al-Shamāʾil* (no. 225) of the ḥadīth of Hind bin Abī Hālah—God be pleased with him.

18 This alludes to the case of the Companion, Abū Jandal ibn Suhayl ibn ʿAmr, who escaped to Madīnah from the Quraysh of Makkah, but who then was returned by the Muslims to the polytheists in order to honour the terms of the treaty of Hudaybiyah (see *Itḥāf*, 7:100).

19 Related by Muslim (no. 1817) from ʿĀʾishah—God be pleased with her.

20 Related by al-Bukhārī (no. 3173) and Muslim (no. 1669), and the one who was murdered was ʿAbdullāh ibn Sahl al-Anṣārī—God be pleased with him.

21 Related by al-Bukhārī (no. 4101) of the ḥadīth of Jābir—God be pleased with him.

22 Related by Ibn al-Mubārak in *al-Zuhd* (no. 571) on the authority of al-Awzāʿī, and by Muslim (no. 2052).

23 Related by Muslim (no. 2044) of the ḥadīth of Anas—God be pleased with him.

24 Related by al-Tirmidhī (no. 1829) of the ḥadīth of Ummu Salamah—God be pleased with her.

25 Related by al-Bukhārī (no. 5416) and Muslim (no. 2970) of the ḥadīth of ʿĀʾishah—God be pleased with her.

26 As related by al-Bukhārī (no. 5431), and Muslim (no. 1474) of the ḥadīth of ʿĀʾishah—God be well-pleased with her.

some milk without bread he made do with it,[27] and if he found some melons or fresh dates he ate them.[28] He did not eat while reclining nor at a table,[29] and his serviette was the soles of his feet.[30] He never sated himself with wheat bread for three days successively until the day he went to meet his Lord, simply as a habit he preferred for himself, driven to it neither by poverty nor miserliness.[31]

He responded to invitations to wedding feasts, visited the ill,[32] attended funerals,[33] and walked about in the midst of his enemies without a bodyguard.[34] He was the most unpretentious of people, the most serene without self-importance,[35] the most eloquent without being loquacious,[36] and the most fine-looking of humankind.[37] Nothing of the affairs of the world caused him to be perturbed.[38]

He wore whatever clothing was at hand, sometimes a cloak, sometimes a garment of Yemeni striped-cloth, and sometimes a woolen gown. Whatever was available that was permissible he wore

---

27 As related by al-Bukhārī (no. 211) and Muslim (no. 358) of the ḥadīth of Ibn ʿAbbās—God be pleased with them both.

28 Related by Abū Dāwūd (no. 3838), al-Tirmidhi (no. 1843) and al-Nasāʾī in *al-Sunan al-Kubrā* (no. 6687) of the ḥadīth of ʿĀʾishah—God be pleased with her.

29 or a kind of raised tray.

30 Related by al-Bukhārī (no. 5457) of the statement of Jābir ibn ʿAbdullāh—God be pleased with them both.

31 A case of that noble habit of the refined spirit now termed by some as 'voluntary poverty'.

32 Like his visiting of Saʿd Ibn ʿUbādah—God be pleased with him—as related in al-Bukhārī (no. 4566) and Muslim (no. 1798).

33 Related by al-Tirmidhī in *al-Shamāʾil* (no. 332) of the ḥadīth of Anas—God be pleased with him.

34 Related by al-Tirmidhī (no. 3046) of the ḥadīth of ʿĀʾishah—God be pleased with her.

35 Related by Abū al-Ḥasan ibn al-Daḥḥāk in *al-Shamāʾil* of the ḥadīth of Abū Saʿīd al-Khudrī regarding the Prophet—God bless him and grant him peace—as being humble without being lowly or undignified; and similarly in al-Nasāʾī (no. 1414).

36 As related by al-Bukhārī (no. 3568) and Muslim (no. 2493) of the ḥadīth of ʿĀʾishah—God be pleased with her.

37 Related by al-Tirmidhī in *al-Shamāʾil* (no. 351) of the ḥadīth of Alī—God be pleased with him.

38 Related by Aḥmad in *al-Musnad* (6:69) of the ḥadīth of ʿĀʾishah—God be pleased with her.

it.[39] His signet ring was made of silver,[40] which he wore on the little finger of his right hand, and sometimes his left hand.[41]

He would seat his servant or others behind him on the same mount.[42] He would ride whatever mount was available, sometimes a horse,[43] sometimes a camel,[44] other times a grey mule[45] or a donkey. Sometimes he would walk barefooted wearing neither cloak nor turban nor *qalansuwah*,[46] visiting the sick at the farthest outskirts of the town.[47]

He loved perfumes and disliked foul odors.[48] He kept company with the impoverished[49] and ate with the poor.[50] He would honor the people of virtue for their virtuous character, and win over the people of rank by showing benevolence towards them.[51] He maintained the ties of kinship with his kinsfolk without showing preference for them over others who were more virtuous than them.[52]

He did not treat anyone harshly,[53] and accepted the excuse of those

---

39 Related by al-Bukhārī (nos. 1277, 5799, 5812) and Muslim (nos. 274, 2079) of the ḥadīth of Anas and al-Mughīrah—God be pleased with them both.

40 As related by al-Bukhārī (no. 65) and Muslim (no. 2092) of the ḥadīth of Anas—God be pleased with him.

41 Related by Muslim (nos. 2094, 2095) of the ḥadīth of Anas—God be pleased with him.

42 As related by al-Bukhārī (no. 544).

43 Related by al-Bukhārī (no. 2627) and Muslim (no. 2307).

44 Related by al-Bukhārī (no. 2734).

45 Related by al-Bukhārī (no. 2764), and Muslim (no. 1776).

46 A tall, circular headgear that does not form into a cone; this passage means that he was attired very simply.

47 As related by Muslim (no. 965).

48 Related by al-Nasāʾī (7:61) of the ḥadīth of Anas—God be pleased with him, and Abū Dāwūd (no. 4074) on the authority of ʿĀʾishah—God be pleased with her.

49 Related by Abū Dāwūd (no. 3666) of the ḥadīth of Abū Saʿīd al-Khudrī—God be pleased with him.

50 Related by al-Bukhārī (no. 6452) of the statement of Abū Hurayrah—God be pleased with him.

51 Related by al-Tirmidhī in *al-Shamāʾil* (no. 336) of the ḥadīth of ʿAlī—God ennoble his countenance, and al-Ṭabarānī in *al-Kabīr* (2:304).

52 Related by al-Ḥakīm in *al-Mustadrak* (3:324) of the ḥadīth of Ibn ʿAbbās—God be pleased with them both, and al-Bukhārī (no. 466), Muslim (no. 2382) of the ḥadīth of Abū Saʿīd al-Khudrī—God be pleased with him.

53 Related by Abū Dāwūd (no. 4182) of the ḥadīth of Anas—God be pleased with him—and al-Tirmidhī in *al-Shamāʾil* (no. 344) of the ḥadīth of ʿAmr ibn ʿĀṣ—God be pleased with him.

who pleaded with him.[54] He jested but only said what was true,[55] and laughed without guffawing.[56] He would watch permissible pastimes without showing disapproval, and he would race with his wives. Voices would be raised around him but he exhibited forbearance.[57]

He had some milch camels and goats from which he provided himself and his family with milk.[58] He owned a bondsman and a bondswoman, and yet he did not enjoy better food or clothing than them.[59] Not a moment of his time would pass him by except he was doing some service for God Most High, or was engaged in what was indispensable for the maintenance of his own self;[60] and he would go out to the orchards of his Companions.

He did not demean the poor because of their poverty or hardship, and he was not awed by kings because of their dominion. Rather, he invited this and that person to God—glorified and exalted be He—with the same invitation without favoritism.[61]

God Most High has indeed gathered for him a virtuous life and a complete governance of affairs, even though he was unlettered, neither reading nor writing, and brought up in the land of ignorance and desert in the midst of poverty and shepherding, an orphan with neither father nor mother. However, God Most High educated him in all the nobilities of good character and praiseworthy manners, and taught him the accounts of the ancients and the moderns, and

---

54 Related by al-Bukhārī (no. 4418) and Muslim (no. 2769).

55 Related by al-Tirmidhī (no. 1990) of the ḥadīth of Abū Hurayrah—God be pleased with him.

56 Related by al-Bukhārī (no. 4829), and Muslim (no. 899) of the ḥadīth of ʿĀʾishah—God be pleased with her.

57 As related by Ibn Ḥazm in *Jawāmiʿ al-Sīrah* (p. 35), and by al-Bukhārī (no. 4367); see also *Itḥāf* (7:106).

58 Related in al-Bukhārī (no. 4194) of the ḥadīth of Salamah ibn al-Akwaʿ—God be pleased with him, and Abū Dāwūd (no. 142) of the ḥadīth of Laqīṭ ibn Ṣabrah, and Ibn Saʿd in *al-Ṭabaqāt* (1:425) of the ḥadīth of Umm Salamah—God be pleased with her.

59 Related by Ibn Saʿd in *al-Ṭabaqāt* (1:428) of the ḥadīth of Salmā—God be pleased with her.

60 Related by al-Tirmidhī in *al-Shamāʾil* (no. 336) of the ḥadīth of ʿAlī—God ennoble his countenance.

61 Related by al-Bukhārī (no. 5091) of the ḥadīth of Sahl ibn Saʿd—God be pleased with him, and Muslim (no. 1774) of the ḥadīth of Anas—God be pleased with him.

instructed him about matters wherein is found salvation and success in the Afterlife and felicity and deliverance in this worldly life, as well as devotion to what is indispensable and relinquishment of what is superfluous.

May God facilitate for us the path to obeying him in what he commands and to emulating him in what he does. Amen! Amen! O Lord of all the Worlds.[62]

62 See also *Jawāmiʿ al-Sīrah* (pp. 34-35) by al-Imām Ibn Ḥazm.

3

An Account of Some Other Aspects of His Comportment and Character (God Bless Him and Grant Him Peace)

Of that which Abū al-Bakhtarī reported: "They said that God's Messenger—God bless him and grant him peace—did not reproach any believer except that it was made an atonement and a mercy for him."[1] And he never once cursed a woman or a servant.[2] It was said to him when he was in the midst of battle, "Would that you curse them, O God's Messenger!" To which he—blessings and peace be on him—said, "I was only sent as a mercy, and I was not sent as a curser."[3]

And when he was asked to pray against someone, Muslim or disbeliever, commoner or elite, he would avert from praying against him to praying for him.[4] He never once hit anyone with his hand except when he was fighting in the path of God Most High. He did not at all avenge himself for something done to him except when it infringed upon what was prohibited by God. He never chose between two matters except that he always chose what was easier, unless it involved a sin or the rending of kinship ties, in which case

1 That is, for the one reproached; related by al-Bukhārī (no. 6361), Muslim (no. 2601) of the ḥadīth of Abū Hurayrah—God be pleased with him.

2 Related by al-Bukhārī (no. 6038), and Muslim (no. 2309), of the ḥadīth of Anas—God be pleased with him.

3 Related by Muslim (no. 2599).

4 Related by al-Bukhārī (no. 2937) and Muslim (no. 2524) of the ḥadīth of Abū Hurayrah—God be pleased with him.

he would be the most removed of people from that.[5] None would come to him, whether free-born, male slave or female slave, except he would provide assistance to them in their need.[6]

Anas—God be well-pleased with him—said, "By Him who sent him with the Truth, he never once told me about something he disliked, 'Why did you do that?' And none would censure me from among his womenfolk except that he would say, 'Leave him alone, for this is already written and preordained.'"[7]

They said, "He—God bless him and grant him peace—never complained about his bedding. If they spread it out for him he would lie down on it, and if it was not spread out for him he would lie down on the ground."[8]

God Most High described him—in the first line of the Torah before He sent him—saying, "Muḥammad is the Messenger of God, My chosen servant. He is not coarse, harsh nor clamorous in the market-places. He does not requite evil with evil but he forgives and pardons. His birthplace is in Makkah, his emigration is to Ṭābah,[9] and his kingdom is in the Levant. He covers his midriff. He and those with him are callers to the Qurʾān and knowledge. He makes ablution of his limbs."[10] And he is likewise described in the *Injīl* (Gospel).[11]

It is of his moral character that he would initiate greetings of peace to whomever he met.[12] If a person pressed him with some need, he would bear patiently with him until he took his leave.[13] When someone took his hand in greeting, he would not release his

---

5 Related by al-Bukhārī (no. 6126), and Muslim (no. 2327), of the ḥadīth of ʿAʾishah—God be pleased with her.

6 Related by al-Bukhārī (no. 6072) and Ibn Mājah (no. 4177).

7 Related by Ahmad in *al-Musnad* (3:231).

8 It is known, as related by al-Tirmidhī (no. 2377) that the Prophet—God bless him and grant him peace—slept on a mat, which left marks on him when he stood up; and that he was not prone to finding faults with things; see *Itḥāf* (7:108).

9 That is, Madīnah.

10 Related by al-Dārimī in his *Musnad* (nos. 5, 7) on the authority of Kaʿb al-Aḥbār.

11 Related by Ibn Saʿd in his *Ṭabaqāt* (1:312) of the ḥadīth of ʿAʾīshah.

12 Related by al-Tirmidhī in *al-Shamāʾil* (no. 8) of the ḥadīth of Hind ibn Abī Hālah—God be pleased with him.

13 Related by Ibn Saʿd in his *Ṭabaqāt* (1:362-365). and al-Tirmidhī in *al-Shamāʾil* (no. 336), of the ḥadīth of ʿAlī—God ennoble his countenance,

hand until the other person did so.[14] And whenever he met anyone of his Companions he would initiate shaking hands with him,[15] taking his hand, clasping it and gripping it firmly.[16]

He did not rise or sit except by mentioning God Most High.[17] Nobody would be sitting in his company while he was praying except he would shorten his prayer and then face him and say, "Do you have a need?" When the person's need was satisfied he returned to his prayer.[18]

When he sat, most often he would sit by drawing up his legs and holding them together with his two hands as though having them wrapped in his garment.[19] His sitting place could not be told apart from the sitting places of his Companions, for he would be sitting at the periphery of the gathering.[20]

He was never seen stretching out his legs among his Companions and thereby constricting the space of anyone of them unless there was ample room with no constriction.[21] And most often he would be sitting facing towards the direction of prayer.[22]

He would show regard for the person who visited him to the extent that he would spread out his cloak for the visitor who was not his relative or foster brother, and sit him upon it.[23] And he would

---

14 Related by al-Tirmidhī (no. 2490) and Ibn Mājah (no. 3716).

15 Related by Abū Dāwūd (no. 5614).

16 Related by ʿAbdullāh ibn Wahb in his *al-Jāmiʿ fī al-Ḥadīth* (no. 182) of the ḥadīth of Hudhayfah ibn al-Yaman—God be pleased with him—and al-Hākim in *Maʿrifah ʿUlūm al-Ḥadīth* (p. 33).

17 Related by al-Tirmidhī in *al-Shamāʾil* (no. 336) of the ḥadīth of ʿAlī—God ennoble his countenance.

18 Related by Aḥmad in his *Musnad* (3:500), and al-Bukhārī (no. 706) of the ḥadīth of Anas—God be pleased with him.

19 Related by al-Bukhārī (no. 6272) of the ḥadīth of Ibn ʿUmar—God be pleased with them both—and Abū Dāwūd (no. 4846) of the ḥadīth of Abū Saʿīd al-Khudrī—God pleased with him.

20 Related by Abū Dāwūd (no. 4698) and al-Nasāʾī (8:101) of the ḥadīth of Abū Dharr and Abū Hurayrah— God be pleased with them both.

21 Related by Abū Nuʿaym in *al-Hilyah* (9:250) of the ḥadīth of Jābir—God be pleased with him; and by al-Tirmidhī (no. 2490) and Ibn Mājah (no. 3716) of the ḥadīth of Anas—God be pleased with him.

22 Related by al-Kharāʾiṭī in *Makārim al-Akhlāq* (no. 749) of the ḥadīth of Ibn ʿUmar—God be pleased with them both.

23 Related by al-Kharāʾiṭī in *Makārim al-Akhlāq* (no. 726) of the ḥadīth of Anas—God be pleased with him.

give preference to his visitor for the use of the cushion he sat on, and if the visitor declined, he would bear on him until he accepted. None befriended him except that the person believed himself to be the noblest of people to him. This was because he would give each one who sat with him his share of his attention, so much so that it was as if his company, listening, talking, graceful conviviality and attentiveness were all for his visitor, and yet, for all that, his company was decorous, unpretentious, humble and honest.[24] God Most High said, "*So it is because of mercy from God that you were mild towards them; had you been harsh and hard-hearted they would have certainly dispersed from around you.*"[25]

He would call his Companions by their paedonymies[26] to honor and to incline their hearts,[27] or bestow paedonymies to those who did not have them, and so a Companion would be called by the paedonymy he gave them.[28] He would also give paedonymies to women who had children, and as for those who bore no children he would invent paedonymies for them.[29] He also gave paedonymies to children in order that their hearts thereby be softened.[30]

He was the most removed of people from anger, and the quickest of them to please.[31] He was the kindest of people towards people, the best of people in showing goodness towards people, and the most helpful of people towards people.[32] In his council, voices were not raised.[33] When he stood up from his council he would say, "O

---

24 Related by al-Tirmidhī in *al-Shamāʾil* (no. 344) of the ḥadīth of ʿAmr ibn ʿĀṣ—God be pleased with him.

25 Qurʾān, *Āl ʿImrān*, 3:159.

26 i.e., referring to parents by the names of their children.

27 Related by al-Bukhārī (no. 3653), Muslim (no. 2381), al-Ḥākim in *al-Mustadrak* (3:223) and al-Ṭabarānī in *al-Kabīr* (9:65).

28 Related by al-Tirmidhī (no. 3830), Ibn Mājah (no. 3738) and al-Ḥākim in *al-Mustadrak* (4:278).

29 Related by al-Ḥākim in *al-Mustadrak* (4:63), Ibn Mājah (no. 3739), and Abū Dāwūd (no.4970).

30 Related by al-Bukhārī (no. 6129) and Muslim (no. 2150) of the ḥadīth of Anas—God be pleased with him.

31 Related by al-Tirmidhī (no. 2191) of the ḥadīth of Abū Saʿīd al-Khudrī; see *Itḥāf* (7:111).

32 Related by Ibn ʿAsākir in *Tārīkh Dimashq* (54:197) of the ḥadīth of ʿAlī—God ennoble his countenance.

33 Related by al-Tirmidhī in *al-Shamāʾil* (no. 336) of the ḥadīth of ʿAlī—God ennoble

God! Be Thou sanctified and praised; I bear witness that there is no god but Thou; I seek Thy forgiveness and I repent to Thee." Then he said, "Jibrīl—on whom be peace—has taught me these words."[34]

his countenance.

34 Related by al-Nasāʾī in *al-Yaum waʾl-Laylah* (p.320, no. 426), and al-Ḥākim in *al-Mustadrak* (1:721, no. 1972), of the ḥadīth of Rāfiʿ ibn Khudayj (see *Iḥyāʾ*, Dār al-Fayḥāʾ ed., 3:457 n.3).

4

An Account of His Speech and Laughter (God Bless Him and Grant Him Peace)

He—God bless him and grant him peace—was the most eloquent of people in speech, and the pleasantest of them in conversation.[1] He said, "I am the most eloquent of the Arabs."[2] Indeed the people of the Garden converse there in the language of Muḥammad—God bless him and grant him peace.[3]

He was succinct in his speech and considerate in his statement. When he spoke he was not garrulous, and it was as if his speech were like a string of pierced pearls.[4] ʿĀʾishah—God be well-pleased with her—said, "He did not converse in his speech the way you do; his speech was laconic while you render yours so prosaic."[5]

They said, "He was the most concise of people in speech, for Jibrīl came to him in that manner of speech; and notwithstanding that conciseness he was able to gather all that he wanted to say, for he would speak words of comprehensive meaning with neither

1 Related by al-Ḥāfiẓ al-Silafī in *Muʿjam al-Safar* (no. 1103) of the ḥadīth of Buraydah—God be pleased with him.

2 Related by Ibn al-Aʿrābī in his *Muʿjam* (no. 2408) on the authority of al-Ḥasan, and al-Ṭabarānī in *al-Kabīr* (6:35, no. 5337), and Abū al-Nuʿaym in *Maʿrifat al-Ṣaḥabah* (3:1262) of the ḥadīth of Abū Saʿīd al-Khudrī, and al-Ḥākim in *Maʿrifat ʿUlūm al-Ḥadīth* (p. 116) of the ḥadīth of ʿUmar—God be pleased with him.

3 Related by Ibn Abī al-Dunyā in *Ṣifat al-Jannah* (nos. 218, 219) of the ḥadīth of Ibn ʿAbbās.

4 Related by Ibn Saʿd in *al-Ṭabaqāt* (1:196-198), and al-Ṭabarānī in *al-Kabīr* (4:94).

5 Related by al-Bukhārī (no. 3568) and Muslim (no. 2493) and Ibn Abī al-Dunyā in *al-Ṣumt wa Adab al-Lisān* (no. 733).

surfeit nor deficit. His speech was such that its parts cohered with one another, and it was interspersed with pauses so that the listener could follow and understand it."[6] He had a clearly audible voice,[7] and he was the finest of people in cadence.[8]

He would be long silent, not speaking without need[9] nor saying anything wrong. He would only say what the truth was, whether he was pleased or angry.[10] He would turn away from anyone speaking inappropriately,[11] and express himself metonymically[12] whenever he had to say anything unpleasant.[13] When he was silent the people in his gathering would speak, and none would be arguing in his presence.[14] He would admonish in all earnestness and by giving good counsel.[15] He said, "Do not allow a part of the Qurʾān to contradict another,[16] for it has been revealed in various aspects."[17]

He was the most smiling and laughing of people in the presence of his Companions, and most full of wonderment at what they discussed, thoroughly engaging himself with them.[18] At times he laughed till

---

6 Related by al-Dāruquṭnī in his *Sunan* (4:144) of the ḥadīth of Ibn ʿAbbās—God be pleased with them both; and by al-Bukhārī (no. 2977) and Muslim (no. 523).

7 Related by al-Tirmidhī (no. 3535) and al-Nasāʾī in *al-Kubrā* (no. 11,114) of the ḥadīth of Ṣafwān ibn ʿAssāl.

8 Related by al-Bukhārī (no. 769) and Muslim (no. 464) of the ḥadīth of al-Barrā Ibn ʿAzib—God be pleased with him.

9 Related by al-Tirmidhī in *al-Shamāʾil* (no. 225) of the ḥadīth of Hind ibn Abī Hālah.

10 Related by Abū Dāwūd (no. 3646) of the ḥadīth of ʿAbdullāh ibn ʿAmr—God be pleased with them both.

11 Related by al-Tirmidhī in *al-Shamāʾil* (no. 351) of the ḥadīth of ʿAlī—God ennoble his countenance.

12 i.e., allusively rather than explicitly.

13 Related by al-Bukhārī (no. 2639), and Muslim (no. 1433), of the ḥadīth of ʿĀʾishah—God be well-pleased with her.

14 Related by al-Tirmidhī in *al-Shamāʾil* (no. 351), of the ḥadīth of ʿAlī—God ennoble his countenance.

15 Related by Muslim (no. 867), of the ḥadīth of Jābir—God be pleased with him.

16 Related by al-Bukhārī (no. 2419) and Muslim (no. 818).

17 I.e., do not read or understand the Qurʾān in a manner such that the meaning of some of it verses are made to contradict the meaning of some other verses, for the Qurʾān, as a whole, is coherent in meaning and the truth of its verses are mutually reinforcing; see Ibn Saʿd in *al-Ṭabaqāt* (4:179), and Aḥmad in *al-Musnad* (2:185).

18 Related by al-Tirmidhī in *al-Shamāʾil* (no. 351), of the ḥadīth of ʿAlī—God ennoble his countenance.

his wisdom teeth showed.[19] The laughter of his Companions in his presence was a smile in imitation of him and out of regard for him.

They said, "A Bedouin came to him one day while he—God bless him and grant him peace—had an altered complexion that his Companions could not comprehend. The Bedouin wanted to pose a question to him, but they said, 'Do not do so, O Bedouin, for we do not understand his complexion.'[20] He responded, 'Let me be. By Him Who has sent him in truth as a Prophet, I will not let him be until he smiles.' And so he said, 'O God's Messenger! It has reached us that the Anointed—that is, the Anti-Christ—will come to people with some broth of meat and bread while they are dying of starvation. Do you view—my parents be your ransom—that I should abstain from his broth out of reticence and decency until I perish out of emaciation, or that I partake of his broth until I am thoroughly sated, after which I would believe in God and deny him?'" They said, "Thereupon God's Messenger—God bless him and grant him peace—laughed such that his wisdom teeth showed. Then he said, 'No. Rather, God will enrich you with that with which He enriches the believers.'"[21]

They said, "He was among the most smiling of people and the most pleasant of them in personality so long as a Qurʾānic revelation was not being sent down to him,[22] or he was not mentioning the Last Hour,[23] or delivering a sermon of admonition,[24] or the time for prayer was not nigh,[25] or an impediment had not cropped up."[26]

And when he rejoiced and was pleased he would be the most elated of people; and when he admonished he would do so very earnestly. And when he was angered—and he would not be angered except for the sake of God—nothing could withstand his anger.

---

19 Related by al-Bukhārī (no. 1936) and Muslim (no. 1111).

20 I.e., his mood or frame of mind.

21 Related by al-Ābī in *Nathr al-Durr* (2:133).

22 Related by al-Ṭabarānī in *Makārim al-Akhlāq* (no. 22) on the authority of Jābir—God be pleased with him.

23 Related by al-Nasāʾī (3:188) of the ḥadīth of Jābir—God be pleased with him.

24 Related by Muslim (no. 867) of the ḥadīth of Jābir—God be pleased with him.

25 Related by al-Bukhārī (no. 676), of the ḥadīth of ʿĀʾishah—God be pleased with her.

26 Related by al-Bukhārī (no. 3206), and Muslim (no. 899), of the ḥadīth of ʿĀʾishah—God be pleased with her.

Thus he was in all his affairs.[27]

When some matter befell him, he consigned the affair to God, relinquished his strength and power, and beseeched Him for guidance. He would say, "O God! Show me the truth as truth that I may follow it, and show me falsehood as falsehood and bestow on me its avoidance. Protect me from being confused lest I follow my inclinations without guidance from You. Render my inclinations in accord with obedience to You. Let Yourself be pleased with myself in wellbeing. Guide me, by Your leave, in regard to any matter that is disagreed therein as to the truth, for You most surely guide whomsoever You will unto a straight path."[28]

27 Related by al-Bukhārī (no. 3556), and Muslim (no. 2769), of the ḥadīth of Kaʿb—God be pleased with him.

28 Related by Muslim (no. 770) of the ḥadīth of ʿĀʾishah—God be pleased her; and Abū Nuʿaym in *Tārīkh Iṣbahān* (2:90) and Ibn ʿAsākir in *Tārīkh Dimashq* (2:369), of the ḥadīth of Abū Hurayrah—God be well-pleased with him.

5

An Account of His Ethics and Comportment in Regard to Food (God Bless Him and Grant Him Peace)

He—God bless him and grant him peace—would eat whatever was available. The most desired of food for him was that which was on the *ḍafaf*; and the *ḍafaf* is that which is partaken of by many hands.[1] When food was served he would say, "In the name of God; O God! Make this a blessing for which gratitude is shown, and through which is attained the blessing of the Garden."[2]

When he sat down to eat, he would often join his knees and feet just as a worshipper would do, except that one knee would be over the other knee, and one foot over the other foot, and he would say, "Verily I am a slave; I eat as a slave eats, and I sit as a slave sits."[3] He would not eat hot food, regarding which he would say, "Indeed, it has no blessing, for God did not feed us fire, therefore cool it;"[4]

---

1 Related by Aḥmad in *al-Musnad* (3:270), of the ḥadīth of Anas—God be pleased with him; and likewise by al-Tirmidhī in *al-Shamāʾil* (no. 72), on the authority of Mālik ibn Dīnār.

2 al-ʿIrāqī says that the part on mentioning God's name is related by al-Nasāʾī, while the rest of the ḥadīth is unknown to him (*Itḥāf*, 7:115).

3 Related by ʿAbd al-Razzāq in *al-Muṣannaf* (10:415), and ibn al-Ḍaḥḥāk in *al-Shamāʾil*, Abū al-Shaykh in *al-Akhlāq*, and al-Bazzār, and Abū Yaʿlā; see also *Itḥāf* (7:116).

4 Related by al-Ḥākim in *al-Mustadrak* (4:118), of the ḥadīth of Jābir—God be pleased with him; and al-Ṭabarānī in *al-Awsaṭ* (no. 7008), of the ḥadīth of Abū Hurayrah—God be pleased with him.

and he would eat from what was near him.[5] He ate with three of his fingers[6] and sometimes he used a fourth finger,[7] but he would not eat with two fingers, regarding which he would say, "Such is indeed Satan's way of eating."[8]

ʿUthmān ibn ʿAffān—God be well-pleased with him—visited him bringing a sweetmeat,[9] and he ate from it, and said, "What is this, O father of ʿAbdullāh?" He said, "My father and mother be your ransom; we put butter and honey in the cooking pot, then we placed it on the fire and we boiled it, then we took the best portion of the wheat when it was ground and sprinkled it over the butter and honey in the cooking pot, and then we stirred it until it was well cooked, and the result is what you see." God's Messenger—God bless him and grant him peace—said, "This food is indeed wholesome."[10]

He used to eat bread of unsieved barley.[11] He would eat cucumbers with dates,[12] and with some salt.[13] The most favored of fresh fruits to him were melons and grapes.[14] He used to eat melons with bread and sugar,[15] and sometimes he ate them with dates; and he would make use of both his hands.[16]

One day he was eating some dates in his right hand while keeping the date stones in his left hand. A sheep passed by, and he showed

---

5 As related in al-Bukhārī (no. 5376), and Muslim (no. 2022).

6 As related by Muslim (no. 2032).

7 As related by Abū Bakr al-Shāfiʿī in *al-Ghaylāniyyāt* (no. 961).

8 As related by al-Ṭabarānī in *al-Kabīr* (11:126), of the ḥadīth of Ibn ʿAbbās—God be pleased with him.

9 Called *fālūdhaj*, made of flour and honey.

10 Related by al-Bayhaqī in *Shuʿab al-Īmān* (no. 5532), of the ḥadīth of Layth ibn Abī Sulaym; and by Ibn Mājah (no. 3340) of the ḥadīth of Ibn ʿAbbās—God be pleased with them both.

11 As related in al-Bukhārī (no. 5413).

12 As related in al-Bukhārī (no. 5440), and Muslim (no. 2043).

13 According to al-Ḥāfiẓ al-ʿIrāqī, this part is related by Abū al-Shaykh, and Ibn ʿAdī (details in *Itḥāf*, 7:118).

14 Related by Abū Dāwūd (no. 3836), and al-Tirmidhi (no. 1843), of the ḥadīth of ʿĀʾishah—God be pleased with her.

15 al-Ḥāfiẓ al-ʿIrāqī says that he does not know a ḥadīth on this fact, but that there is a weak ḥadīth on him eating grapes with bread (see *Itḥāf*, 7:118).

16 Related by Ahmad in *al-Musnad* (1:204), of the hadith of ʿAbdullāh ibn Jaʿfar—God be pleased with him. al-Ḥāfiẓ al-ʿIrāqī says that most probably he used his right hand to take what was held in his left hand and ate it with what was in his right hand (see *Itḥāf*, 7:119).

it the date stones, whereupon it began to eat them out of his left hand while he ate with his right hand until he finished eating and the sheep left.[17] He would sometimes eat grapes by stripping their stalks bare of them,[18] such that the froth on his beard appeared as pierced pearls, which were the juice that flowed in drops off him. Most of his food consisted of water and dried dates.[19] He used to combine milk with dried dates and called them the two most wholesome ones.[20]

The most beloved of food to him was meat,[21] and he used to say, "It improves the sense of hearing; and it is the chief of foods in this world and the Hereafter. If I had asked my Lord to feed me with it every day He would have done so."[22] He used to eat soup with meat and pumpkins.[23] He loved pumpkins and said, "It is the tree of my brother, Yūnus—peace be on him."[24]

ʿĀʾishah—God be well-pleased with her—said, "He used to say, 'O ʿĀʾishah, when you cook in the pot put in plenty of gourds, for they fortify the heart of the distressed.'"[25] He used to eat the meat of birds that were hunted,[26] but he did not track the bird nor hunt it. Rather, he preferred that it be hunted for him and brought to him, and then he ate it.[27]

When he ate meat, he did not incline his head toward it. Instead,

---

17 Related by Abū Bakr al-Shāfiʿī in *al-Ghaylāniyyāt* (no. 986) of the ḥadīth of Anas—God be pleased with him.

18 Related by al-Ṭabarānī in *al-Kabīr* (12:149), and al-Bayhaqī in *Shuʿab al-Īmān* (no. 5565).

19 Related by al-Bukhārī (no. 5383), of the ḥadīth of ʿĀʾishah —God be pleased with her.

20 Related by Aḥmad in *al-Musnad* (3:474).

21 Related by al-Tirmidhī in *al-Shamāʾil* (no. 179), of the ḥadīth of Jābir (see *Itḥāf*, 7:119).

22 Related by Ibn Mājah (no. 3305), of the ḥadīth of Abū Dardāʾ (see *Itḥāf*, 7:119).

23 Related by al-Bukhārī (no. 2092), and Muslim (no. 2041), of the ḥadīth of Anas—God be pleased with him.

24 Related by al-Bukhārī (no. 2092), and Muslim (no. 2041), of the ḥadīth of Anas—God be pleased with him.

25 Related by Abū Bakr al-Shāfiʿī in *al-Ghaylāniyyāt* (no. 957).

26 Related by Abū Dāwūd (no. 3797), and al-Tirmidhī (no. 1828), of the ḥadīth of Safīnah—God be pleased with him.

27 As apparent in what is related by Abū Dāwūd (no. 2859), al-Tirmidhī (no. 2257), and al-Nasāʾī (7:195), of the hadith of Ibn ʿAbbās—God be pleased with him.

he would bring it up to his mouth and then he would bite into it with his front teeth.[28] He used to eat bread with butter.[29] Of sheep, he liked the forearm and shoulder; and of what is cooked in the cooking pot he liked gourds. Of seasoning he loved vinegar, and of dried dates he loved the *ʿajwah* dates.[30] He prayed for blessedness in the *ʿajwah*,[31] regarding which he said, "It is of the Garden, and a cure for poison and sorcery."[32] Of vegetables he liked the endive,[33] mountain balm, and purslane, which is called *al-rijlah*.[34] He disliked the kidneys because of them being the provenance of urine.[35] He would not eat seven parts of the sheep: the phallus, the testicles, the bladder, the gall bladder, the glands,[36] the vulva,[37] and the blood, for he disliked them.[38] He would also eat neither garlic, onions nor leek.[39]

He never found fault with food. Rather, if it appealed to him he ate it and if he disliked it, he disregarded it, and if he disliked it, he would not render it averse to others. He was averse to the thorn-tail

---

28 Related by Abū Dāwūd (no. 3779), and al-Tirmidhī (no. 1835), of the ḥadīth of Ṣafwān ibn Umayyah; and by al-Bukhārī (no. 3340), and Muslim (no. 194), of the ḥadīth of Abū Hurayrah—God be pleased with him.

29 Related by al-Bukhāri (no. 3578) and Muslim (no. 2040).

30 As related by Abū al-Shaykh in *Akhlāq al-Nabiyy—ṣallallāhu ʿalayhi wassalam—wa Ādābihi* (nos. 594, 602, 626), of the hadith of Ibn ʿAbbās—God be pleased with them. The *ʿajwah* is a special kind of dates grown in Madīnah.

31 Related by Ibn ʿAsākir in *Tārīkh Dimashq* (11:226), of the ḥadīth of Jābir—God be pleased with him.

32 Related by al-Tirmidhī (no. 2066), and al-Nasāʾī in *al-Sunan al-Kubrā* (no. 6636), and Ibn Mājah (no. 3453), of the ḥadīth of Ibn Saʿīd and Jābir—God be pleased with them; and similarly by al-Bukhārī (no. 5445), and Muslim (no. 2047), of the ḥadīth of Saʿd ibn Abī Waqqāṣ—God be pleased with him.

33 Related by Abū al-Qāsim al-Jurjānī in *Tārīkh Jurjān* (1:103), of the ḥadīth of Anas—God be pleased with him.

34 Related by al-Ḥārith ibn Usāmah in his *Zawāʾid* (no. 535), and al-Jurjānī in *Tārīkh Jurjān* (1:242).

35 Related by Ibn Sunnī in the book, *al-Ṭibb al-Nabawī* (see *Itḥāf*, 7:121).

36 Or any lumpy swelling overspread by fat arising in between the skin and the meat beneath.

37 i.e., genitals of female hoofed animals.

38 Related by al-Ṭabarānī in *al-Awsaṭ* (no. 9476), of the ḥadīth of Ibn ʿUmar; and by Ibn ʿAdī in *al-Kāmil* (5:12), of the hadith of Ibn ʿAbbās—God be pleased with them.

39 Related by Muslim (no. 564), and by Abū Nuʿaym in the *Ḥilyah* (6:332).

lizard[40] and the spleen,[41] but he did not declare them forbidden to eat.

He used to wipe the dish with his fingers, saying, "The last morsel of the food contains the most blessing."[42] And he used to lick his fingers clean of food until they turned red.[43] He would not wipe his hand until he had licked his fingers one by one, saying, "Indeed, it is not known on which fingers the blessing is." When he was finished eating he would say, "O my Lord! For You is the praise; You fed and thus You sated; and You gave drink and thus You quenched. For You is the praise undenied, unignored and indispensable."[44]

When he ate bread and, especially, meat, he would wash his hands thoroughly and then wipe his face with the excess water.[45] He used to drink in three portions, invoking the name of God three times, and praising God thrice when he was done.[46]

He would drink water in sips rather than gulp it down.[47] He sometimes drank in one breath until he finished.[48] He would not breathe into the drinking vessel. Rather, he would avoid doing so.[49]

He would give the surplus of his food to the one on his right;[50] and if the person on his left was higher in rank, he would say to the one on his right, "It is *sunnah* (preferred custom) to give it to you, but if you wish you may prefer them (over yourself)."[51]

---

40 Related by al-Bukhārī (no. 5400) and Muslim (no. 1945).

41 Related by Ibn Mājah (no. 3314); and by al-Bayhaqī in *al-Sunan al-Kubrā* (10:7), of the ḥadīth of Zayd ibn Thābit—God be pleased with him.

42 Related by Muslim (no. 2034), of the ḥadīth of Anas—God be pleased with him; and al-Nasāʾī in *al-Sunan al-Kubrā* (no. 6736), of the ḥadīth of Jābir—God be pleased with him.

43 Related by Muslim (no. 2032), of the ḥadīth of Kaʿb—God be pleased with him

44 Related by Aḥmad in *al-Musnad* (4:236); and similarly by al-Bukhārī (no. 5459), of the ḥadīth of Abū Umāmah—God be pleased with him.

45 Related by Abū Yaʿlā in his *Musnad* (no. 5567), of the ḥadīth of Ibn ʿUmar—God be pleased with them.

46 Related by al-Ṭabarānī in *al-Awsaṭ* (no. 844), of the ḥadīth of Abū Hurayrah—God be pleased with him; see also al-Bukhārī (no. 5631) an Muslim (no. 2028).

47 Related by al-Ṭabarānī in *al-Kabīr* (2:47); and by Abu Nuʿaym in *Maʿrifat al-Ṣaḥābah* (1:440).

48 Al-ʿIraqī says this is a weak ḥadīth related by Abū al-Shaykh; for more details, see *Itḥāf*, 7:125.

49 Related by al-Bukhārī (no. 153), of the ḥadīth of Abū Qatādah—God be well-pleased with him.

50 Related by al-Bukhārī (no. 2352) and Muslim (no. 2029).

51 Related by al-Bukhārī (no. 2351), and Muslim (no. 2030), of the ḥadīth of Sahl

A vessel containing honey and milk was brought to him but he declined to drink it, saying, "Two drinks in one drink and two victuals in one dish?" Then he—God bless him and grant him peace—said, "I do not forbid it, but I detest vanity and facing the reckoning for the excesses of the world on the morrow; and I desire humility, for indeed, whoever is humble before God, God will exalt him."[52]

In his household he was more bashful than the *ʿātiq*,[53] for he would not ask them for food, nor would he cause them inconvenience in his desire for it. If they served him food he would eat it. Whatever they brought him he accepted, and whatever they offered him to drink, he drank.[54] He would sometimes arise and take for himself what he wanted to eat or drink.[55]

---

ibn Saʿd—God be well-pleased with him.

52 Related by al-Ṭabarānī in *al-Awsaṭ* (no. 4891), of the ḥadīth of ʿĀʾishah—God be well-pleased with her.

53 A woman who is no longer obliged or dutybound in service to her parents and her husband.

54 Related by Muslim (no. 1153), of the ḥadīth of ʿĀʾishah—God be well-pleased with her.

55 Related by Abū Dāwūd (no. 3857) and al-Tirmidhī (no. 2037), of the ḥadīth of Umm al-Mundhir al-Anṣāriyyah; and by al-Tirmidhī (no. 1892) and Ibn Mājah (no. 3423), of the ḥadīth of Kabshah—God be well-pleased with her.

6

An Account of His Manners and Character in Regard to Attire (God Bless Him and Grant Him Peace)

THE Prophet—God bless him and grant him peace—would wear whatever was available to him, such as a waist-wrapper, an outer garment, a long shirt, a wide-sleeved robe, or some other clothing.[1] He used to find green garments appealing.[2] Most of his clothes were white in color, and he used to say, "Clothe your living in them, and shroud your dead in them."[3]

He used to wear a padded tunic for battle, and also an unpadded one.[4] He had a long-sleeved tunic of silk brocade which he used to wear, and its green color would look becoming on his fair complexion.[5]

All of his garments were gathered up above his ankles, and his

---

1 Related by al-Bukhārī (no. 3108), Muslim (no. 2080), and Aḥmad in *al-Musnad* (6:133), of the ḥadīth of ʿĀʾishah—God be pleased with him.

2 Related by al-Ṭabarānī in *al-Awsaṭ* (no. 5727), of the ḥadīth of Anas—God be pleased with him; and by Abū Dāwūd (no. 4065) and al-Tirmidhī (no. 2812), on the authority of Abū Ramthah.

3 Related by Abū Dāwūd (no. 3878), al-Tirmidhī (no. 994) and Ibn Mājah (no. 1473), of the ḥadīth of Ibn ʿAbbās—God be pleased with them; and by al-Nasāʾī (8:205).

4 That is, when he was not engaged in battle; related by Muslim (no. 2070), of the ḥadīth of Jābir—God be pleased with him.

5 Related by al-Bukhārī (no. 2615); and Aḥmad in *al-Musnad* (3:206, no. 12736), who says this was before the prohibition of wearing silk; *sundus* here can also mean thin or fine textured (Lane's *Arabic-English Lexicon*, s.v. *sundus*).

waist-wrapper would be over them until it reached the middle of his shank.[6] His long shirt was fastened by buttons, but at times he would leave the buttons unfastened during prayer and other occasions.[7] He had a cloak which was dyed with saffron, and occasionally he would lead people in prayer wearing it only.[8] Sometimes he wore a garment only without wearing anything over it.[9] He had a felted garment which he wore,[10] and he used to say, "I am only a slave, I dress as the slave dresses."[11] He had two tunics specifically for his Friday prayer apart from his garments for other occasions.[12] Occasionally he would wear a single waist-wrapper without wearing anything else over it,[13] tying its two ends between his shoulder blades,[14] and so attired he would on occasion lead the people in funeral prayers.[15]

Sometimes he would pray in his house wrapped up in a single waist-wrapper with its two ends bound crosswise; and it would be the same waist-wrapper in which he had conjugal relations that day.[16] Every so often he would pray at night in the waist-wrapper, wearing the part of the garment that was at his side while casting the remainder over his wife, and thus he would pray.[17] He had a

6 Related by al-Ḥāfiẓ Ibn Ṭāhir in *Ṣafwat al-Taṣawwuf* (p. 227), of the ḥadīth of ʿAbdullāh ibn Bisr— God be pleased with him; and by al-Tirmidhī in *al-Shamāʾil* (no. 120), of the ḥadīth of ʿUbayd Ibn Khālid.

7 Related by Abū Dāwūd (no. 4082), and Ibn Mājah (no. 3578), of the ḥadīth of Qurrah ibn Iyyās—God be pleased with him; and by Ibn Khuzaymah in his *Ṣaḥīḥ* (no. 779), of the ḥadīth of Zayd ibn Aslam.

8 Related by al-Tirmidhī (no. 2814), of the ḥadīth of Qaylah bint Makhramah.

9 Related by Ibn Mājah (no. 1032), of the ḥadīth of Thābit Ibn al-Ṣāmit—God be pleased with him.

10 Related by al-Bukhārī (no. 3108), and Muslim (no. 2080); see also *Iḥyāʾ*, Dār al-Fayḥāʾ ed. 3:477n.3.

11 Related by al-Bukhārī (no. 3445), and ʿAbd al-Razzāq in *al-Muṣannaf* (10:415, no. 19543); see also *Iḥyāʾ*, Dār al-Fayḥāʾ ed., 3:477n.4.

12 Related by al-Ṭabarānī in *al-Awsaṭ* (no. 3540), of the ḥadīth of ʿĀʾishah —God be pleased with her.

13 Related by Muslim (no. 1479).

14 Related by al-Bukhārī (no. 352), on the authority of Muḥammad Ibn al-Munkadir.

15 Al-Ḥāfiẓ al-ʿIrāqī says that this report is unknown to him (see *Itḥāf*, 7:128).

16 Related by Abū Yaʿlā in his *Musnad* (no. 7140), of the ḥadīth of Muʿāwiyah—God be pleased with him.

17 Related by Abū Dāwūd (no. 631), of the ḥadīth of ʿĀʾishah—God be pleased with her.

black garment that he gave away to someone, and thereafter Umm Salamah—God be well-pleased with her—said to him, "My father and mother be your ransom! What has become of the black garment?" He said, "I clothed someone in it." She then said, "I never saw anything more becoming than your fair complexion upon its blackness."[18] Anas said, "Sometimes I saw him leading us in the noon prayer attired in a cloak the two ends of which he had tied into a knot."[19]

He used to wear a ring.[20] At times he would go out wearing his ring to which was attached a string by which he would be reminded of things.[21] He would stamp his seal with it on his letters,[22] saying, "The seal on the letter is better than insinuation."[23]

He would wear the round headgear beneath the turban or without the turban. Sometimes he took off his round headgear from his head and rendered it as a guard in front of him toward which he would pray.[24] Occasionally there would be no turban at hand and so he would tie a head-cloth over his head and forehead.[25] He had a turban called *al-Saḥab* (the Cloud) which he gave to ʿAlī. At times ʿAlī would come by wearing it, whereupon the Prophet—God bless him and grant him peace—would say, "ʿAlī comes to you in the Cloud!"[26]

---

18 Related by Abū Dāwūd (no. 4074), of the ḥadīth of ʿĀʾishah—God be pleased with her; al-ʿIrāqī says he is not aware of this being of the ḥadīth of Umm Salamah (see *Itḥāf*, 7:128).

19 Related by Ibn Mājah (no. 3553), of the ḥadīth of ʿUbādah Ibn al-Ṣāmit.

20 Related by al-Bukhārī (no. 65) and Muslim (no. 2092), of the ḥadīth of Anas—God be pleased with him.

21 Related by Ibn ʿAdī in *al-Kāmil* (2:13), of the ḥadīth of Wāthilah ibn al-Asqaʿ—God be pleased with him; and by Ibn Saʿd in his *Ṭabaqāt* (1:333), of the ḥadīth of Ibn ʿUmar—God be pleased with them.

22 Related by al-Bukhārī (no. 65) and Muslim (no. 2092), of the ḥadīth of Anas—God be pleased with him.

23 i.e., better than suspicion and misunderstanding that could happen if it were not sealed; Al-ʿIrāqī says he is unaware of this part of the ḥadīth (see *Itḥāf*, 7:129).

24 Related by Abū al-Shaykh in *Akhlāq al-Nabi sallallāhu alayhi wassalam wa Ādābihi* (no. 302); by al-Bayhaqī in his *Shuʿab* (no. 5848), of the ḥadīth of Ibn ʿUmar—God be well-pleased with them; and by Abū Dāwūd (4078) and al-Tirmidhī (no. 1784), of the ḥadīth of Rukānah—God be pleased with him.

25 Related by al-Bukhārī (no. 927).

26 Related by Ibn ʿAdī in *al-Kāmil* (6:390), and Abū al-Shaykh in *Akhlāq al-Nabi sallallāhu alayhi wassalam wa Ādābihi* (no. 297).

When he put on a tunic, he would put it on from his right side,[27] saying, "All praise be to God Who has dressed me with that by which I conceal my nakedness and by which I adorn myself amongst people."[28] When he took off a tunic, he removed it from his left side.[29] He had a tunic specifically for his Friday prayer apart from his other tunics for other occasions. When he wore a new garment he would give away his old garment to the poor, and say, "There is no Muslim who clothes another Muslim with what is worn out of his garments—and he does so only for God's sake—except that he is within God's security, refuge and goodness as long as the garment covers him whilst living or deceased."[30]

He used to have a mat of leather padded with palm fibers, two cubits in length or thereabouts, and whose breadth was about a cubit and a span.[31] He had a wide outer garment (*ʿabāʿah*) which was spread out for him wherever he moved and folded into two layers beneath him.[32] He used to sleep on a mat with nothing beneath him beside it.[33]

It was his habit to name his beasts of burden, weapons and belongings. The name of his banner was the *al-ʿIqāb* (the Eagle);[34] the name of his sword with which he engaged in battles was *Dhū al-Fiqār*.[35] He had a sword which was called *al-Mikhdham*, and

27 Related by al-Tirmidhī (no. 1766), of the ḥadīth of Abū Hurayrah—God be pleased with him.

28 Related by al-Tirmidhī (no. 3560), and Ibn Mājah (no. 3557), of the ḥadīth of ʿUmar—God be pleased with him.

29 Related by Abū al-Shaykh in *Akhlāq al-Nabi sallallāhu alayhi wassalam wa Ādābihi* (no. 782).

30 Related by al-Ḥākim in *al-Mustadrak* (4:193) and al-Bayhaqī in *Shuʿab al-Īmān* (no. 5873), of the ḥadīth of ʿUmar—God be pleased with him.

31 Related by Muslim (no. 2082), of the ḥadīth of ʿĀʾishah—God be pleased with her; and by Abū al-Shaykh in *Akhlāq al-Nabi sallallāhu alayhi wassalam wa Ādābihi* (no. 462), of the ḥadīth of Umm Salamah—God be pleased with her.

32 Related by Ibn Saʿd in his *Ṭabaqāt* (1:400); and by Abū al-Shaykh in *Akhlāq al-Nabi sallallāhu alayhi wassalam wa Ādābihi* (461), of the ḥadīth of ʿĀʾishah—God be pleased with her.

33 Related by al-Bukhārī (no. 4913) and Muslim (no. 1479), of the ḥadīth of ʿUmar—God be pleased with him.

34 Related by Ibn ʿAdī in *al-Kāmil* (4:291), of the ḥadīth of Abū Hurayrah—God be pleased with him.

35 Related by al-Tirmidhī (no. 1561) and Ibn Mājah (no. 2808), of the ḥadīth of Ibn ʿAbbās—God be pleased with them.

another one which was called *al-Rusūb*, and yet another one which was called *al-Qaḍīb*.[36] The handle of his sword was adorned with silver.[37] He used to wear a belt of leather in which were three rings of silver.[38] The name of his bow was *al-Katūm* (the Unbroken), and the name of his quiver was *al-Kāfūr* (Camphor).[39]

The name of his camel was *al-Qaṣwā*ʾ (the Clipped Ear), and it was she who was also called *al-ʿAḍbā*ʾ (the Slit Ear). The name of his she-mule was *al-Duldul* (the Hedgehog), while the name of his donkey was *Yaʿfūr* (Gazelle). The name of his ewe whose milk he drank was *ʿĪnah* (Favored).[40]

He had a cleansing-vessel of baked clay in which he made ablutions and from which he drank. People would send their young children who had already attained cognitive discernment, and they would enter into the presence of God's Messenger—God bless him and grant him peace. They would not be kept away from him, and thus when they found water in the cleansing-vessel, they would drink from it and wipe it over their faces and bodies, seeking blessings therein.[41]

36 Related by Ibn Saʿd in his *Ṭabaqāt* (1:418), on the authority of Marwān ibn Abī Saʿīd ibn al-Maʿlā.

37 Related by Abū Dāwūd (no. 2583), al-Tirmidhī (no. 1691) and al-Nasāʾī (8:219), of the ḥadīth of Anas—God be well-pleased with him.

38 Related by Ibn Saʿd in his *Ṭabaqāt* (1:419, and 2:35).

39 Related by al-Balādhurī in *Ansāb al-Ashrāf* (2:176).

40 Related by al-Bukhārī (nos. 2734, 2871), Aḥmad in *al-Musnad* (5:238), al-Ṭabarānī in *al-Kabīr* (12:120), and al-Suyūṭī in *al-Shamāʾil al-Sharīfah* (p. 223).

41 al-Ḥāfiẓ al-ʿIrāqī says that the origin (*aṣl*) of this particular report is unknown to him, but that in any case there are widespread reports (*akhbār mutawātirah*) in the two *Ṣaḥīḥ*s and other ḥadīth collections regarding seeking of blessing with water touched by the Prophet—blessing and peace be on him; and as for his special cleansing-vessel, ʿAbdullāh ibn Masʿud—God be well-pleased with him—was known to be keeper (*ṣāḥib*) of his sandals (*al-naʿlayn*), cushion (*al-wisād*) and cleansing-vessel (*al-maṭharah*), as reported in al-Bukhārī (no. 3742).

7

An Account of His Forgiveness (God Bless Him and Grant Him Peace) Notwithstanding His Ability to Censure[1]

THE Messenger of God—God bless him and grant him peace—was the most forbearing of people, and the most eager to forgive notwithstanding his ability to censure. This was so even in the case when some necklaces of gold and silver were brought to him and he proceeded to apportion them among his Companions, whereupon there arose a man of the desert who said, "Oh Muḥammad! By God! Verily God has commanded you to be just, but I do not see you being just." He said, "Woe to you! Who will show you justice after me?" When the man turned away, the Prophet—God bless him and grant him peace—said, "Bring him back to me gently."[2]

Jābir—God be well-pleased with him—related that the Prophet—God bless him and grant him peace—was holding some silver, which was in Bilāl's garment,[3] to be given out to the people on the day of Ḥunayn,[4] when a man said to him, "O Messenger of God, be just!" Whereupon the Prophet—God bless him and grant him peace said, "Woe to you! Who will act justly if I don't act justly? I

1 i.e., his capacity to censure or punish.

2 Related by Abū al-Shaykh in *Akhlāq al-Nabi ṣallallāhu ʿalayhi wassalam wa Ādābihi* (no. 71).

3 The famous Companion—God be well-pleased with him.

4 i.e., on his departure from the battlefield.

would fail and be in loss if I did not act justly." ʿUmar then stood up and said, "O Messenger of God, shall I not strike his neck? For he is a hypocrite." He said, "I seek refuge in God that people should say that I kill my Companions."[5]

The Messenger of God—God bless him and grant him peace—was in a battle when the enemies noticed a moment of heedlessness among the Muslims, whereupon a man advanced brandishing his sword over the head of God's Messenger—God bless him and grant him peace—saying, "Who will defend you against me?" He said, "God," whereupon the sword fell from his hand and God's Messenger grabbed it and said, "Who will defend you against me?" He said, "Be quick with me."[6] He said, "Say: I bear witness that there is no god but God." He said, "No. Rather, I will not fight against you nor be with you, and I will not be with any people who are fighting against you." He let him go his way and then the man went back to his people saying, "I have come back to you from the presence of the best of men."[7]

Anas reported that a Jewish woman brought the Prophet—God bless him and grant him peace—some poisoned mutton that he might perchance eat it, whereupon she was brought to the Prophet—God bless him and grant him peace. He questioned her about it, and she said, "I wished to kill you." He said, "God did not empower you to do so." They said, "Shall we not kill her?" He said, "No."[8]

A Jewish man cast a spell on him and he was informed of it by Jibrīl—upon whom be peace. Thus he drew forth the charm and unraveled its knots, whereupon he felt a lightness.[9] He did not mention the matter to the Jew nor reveal it to him at all.[10]

ʿAlī—God be well-pleased with him—said, "God's Messenger—God bless him and grant him peace—sent for me, Zubayr and

---

5 Related by Muslim (no. 1063) and al-Bukhārī (no. 3610).

6 Or, "Be the better victor," i.e., spare my life.

7 Related by al-Ḥākim in *al-Mustadrak* (3:29), al-Bukhārī (no. 3910), and Muslim (no. 843); and his name was Ghawrath ibn al-Ḥārith and he later on became a Companion.

8 Related by al-Bukhārī (no. 2617), and Muslim (no. 2190). Abū Dāwūd (no. 4512) related she was executed as a legal retribution for the death of Bishr ibn al-Barrāʾ ibn Maʿrūr due to her poisoning, which occurred during the battle of Khaybar.

9 Due to the removal of the sorcery.

10 Related by al-Nasāʾī (7:112), al-Bukhārī (no. 3268), and Muslim (no. 2189).

al-Miqdād, saying, 'Go until you come to Rawḍat Khākh,[11] for a woman in a howdah is there with a letter; take it from her.' So we went off until we reached Rawḍat Khākh and behold, there was the woman. We said, 'Bring forth the letter.' She said, 'I do not have a letter with me.' We said, 'You shall bring forth the letter or we shall take off your clothes,' whereupon she brought it forth from her plaited hair. We took the letter back to the Prophet—God bless him and grant him peace—and behold, it was a message from Ḥāṭib ibn Abī Baltaᶜah to some people of the polytheists of Makkah informing them of a concern among the concerns of God's Messenger—God bless him and grant him peace. He said, 'O Ḥāṭib! What is this?' He said, 'O Messenger of God! Do not be hasty with me. I am a man who was adopted amongst my people,[12] and there are those with you of the Emigrants who have relatives in Makkah protecting their families. I therefore desired, since I lack kin relations with them, that I might have recourse from among them by which they would protect my relatives;[13] and I did not do that out of disbelief or preference for disbelief after having been Muslim or out of apostasy from my religion.' God's Messenger—God bless him and grant him—said, 'You have spoken truthfully.' ᶜUmar—God be well-pleased with him—said, "Allow me that I may strike the neck of this hypocrite." The Prophet—God bless him and grant him peace—said, 'Verily he witnessed (the battle of) Badr, and, for all you know, perhaps God, Mighty, Majestic, has regarded the partisans of Badr and said: Do what you will, for I have forgiven you.'"[14]

The Messenger of God—God bless him and grant him peace—was apportioning some allotments[15] when a man of the Anṣār said, "This apportioning is one by which God's pleasure is not being sought." This was mentioned to the Prophet—God bless him and grant him peace—whereupon his face turned red and he said, "God have mercy

---

11 A place between Madīnah and Makkah.

12 He was a non-Quraʾishite Lakhmi and an ally of the the Quraʾishite clan of Asad ibn ᶜAbd al-ᶜUzzā.

13 The letter warned of the Muslims' impending attack on Makkah, and by thus warning the Makkans, he hoped they would view him in a favorable light and thereby protect his family members who were still residing in Makkah.

14 Related by al-Bukhārī (no. 3007) and Muslim (no. 2494).

15 Distributing war booty to the people.

on my brother Mūsā,[16] for he was hurt by more than this and yet he showed patience."[17]

The Prophet—God bless him and grant him peace—used to say, "Let none of you convey to me anything[18] regarding any one of my Companions, for I would like to go out to you with a sound heart[19]."[20]

16 i.e., the Prophet Mūsā (Moses)—peace be on him.

17 Related by al-Bukhārī (no. 3150) and Muslim (no. 1062).

18 i.e., anything unbecoming regarding them.

19 i.e., without harboring negative perceptions about them.

20 Related by Abū Dāwūd (no. 4860) and al-Tirmidhī (no. 3896).

8

An Account of His Averting of His Gaze from Whatever He Disliked (God Bless Him and Grant Him Peace)

THE Prophet—God bless him and grant him peace—had a fine complexion with a gentle demeanor outwardly and inwardly. His anger and pleasure would be apparent on his countenance. When he was feeling concerned he would stroke his noble beard frequently.[1]

He did not speak directly to a person regarding what he disliked (about him). Once, a man visited him wearing a yellow-colored garment, and he disliked it but did not say anything to him until he went away, whereupon he said to some of the people present, "If only you had told him to desist from it," that is, the color yellow.[2]

A Bedouin urinated in the mosque in his presence and his Companions were agitated by his act, but the Prophet—God bless him and grant him peace—said, "Do not interrupt him." Then he said to him, "These mosques are not appropriate for such defilement, whether urination or excretion." In a narration it says, "Draw people close and do not drive them away."[3]

One day a Bedouin came to him to ask him for something, whereupon the Prophet—God bless him and grant him peace—gave it to him and then he said to him, "Have I done well by you?" The

---

1 Abū al-Shaykh in *Akhlāq al-Nabi sallallāhu alayhi wassalam wa Ādābihi* (no. 104).

2 Related by Abū Dāwūd (no. 4182).

3 Related by al-Bukhārī (nos. 219, 6128), and Muslim (no. 284).

Bedouin responded, "No, nor were you nice." The Muslims were angered and rose against him, but he indicated to them to desist, after which he stood up and went back into his house. Then he sent for the Bedouin and gave him something extra, and said to him, "Have I done good to you?" He replied, "Yes, and may God reward you with wellbeing of family and kinsfolk." The Prophet—God bless him and grant him peace—then said, "You said what you said and something of that has lodged in the hearts of my Companions. Thus, if it would please you, do say in their presence what you just said in my presence so that it would erase from their bosoms what they harbor against you." He said, "Yes."

When it was evening or the next day, the Bedouin came and the Prophet—God bless him and grant him peace—said, "This Bedouin said what he said, but we augmented for him and he maintained that he was satisfied. Isn't that so?" The Bedouin responded, "Yes, and God reward you with wellbeing of family and kinsfolk." Whereupon the Prophet—God bless him and grant him peace—said, "Indeed, the likeness of me and this Bedouin is as the likeness of a man who had a she-camel which ran away from him. The people pursued her but they only chased her further away, and so the master of the she-camel called out to them, 'Leave me and my camel alone, for I am gentler with her and understand her better.' The camel's master then turned to her and faced her directly and brought for her some sweepings of the earth[4] and repeatedly called out to her, '*hui*, *hui*,' until she came and kneeled. Then he fastened her saddle upon her and sat on her. Indeed, had I disregarded you[5] when the man said what he said, and you then killed him, he would have entered the Fire."[6]

4 i.e., some grasses or fodder on the ground.

5 i.e., and not intervened.

6 Related by Abū al-Shaykh in *Akhlāq al-Nabi sallallāhu alayhi wassalam wa Ādābihi* (no. 175).

9

An Account of His Munificence and Generosity (God Bless Him and Grant Him Peace)

THE Prophet—God bless him and grant him peace—was the most generous and munificent of people. During the month of Ramaḍān he was like the free-flowing breeze, withholding nothing.[1]

ʿAlī—God be well-pleased with him—when describing the Prophet—God bless him and grant him peace—would say, "He was the most munificent of all people, the most open-hearted, the most truthful in speech, the most fulfilling of responsibility, the mildest of temperament, the most gracious in companionship, and whosoever unexpectedly saw him became awed by him, and whosoever associated with him, with insight, loved him." He said, describing him, "I have not seen his likeness—God bless him and grant him peace—neither before nor after him."[2]

He was never asked for anything for the sake of Islam but he gave it. Indeed, a man came to him and asked him and he bestowed on him a flock of goats that filled the gap between two hills, whereupon he returned to his people and said, "Accept Islam, for Muḥammad gives as the giving of one who harbors no fear of want."[3] He never

1 Related by al-Bukhārī (no. 6) and Muslim (no. 2308), of the hadith of Ibn Abbās—God be well-pleased with him.

2 Related by al-Tirmidhī (no. 3638) and Abū al-Shaykh in *Akhlāq al-Nabī ṣallallāhu ʿalayhi wassalam wa Ādābihi* (no. 85).

3 Related by Muslim (no. 2312), of the ḥadīth of Anas—God be well-pleased with him.

said, "No," when he was asked for something.[4]

A load of seventy thousand dirhams was brought to him, and he put it down on a mat. He then stood by it and apportioned the coins, and he did not turn away anyone who asked until they were done.[5]

A man came to him asking for something, but he said, "There is nothing with me, but make a purchase on my credit and when something comes our way we will pay for it." ʿUmar said, "O Messenger of God! God has not imposed upon you what you cannot do." The Prophet—God bless him and grant him peace—took a dislike to that, whereupon the man said, "Bestow provisions and harbor no fear of diminishment from God." The Prophet—God bless him and grant him peace—smiled at that, and the joy on his countenance was clearly discernible.[6]

On his return from (the battle of) Ḥunayn, the desert Arabs came to him pressing him with their requests until he was backed up against a tree and his cloak was wrested away from him. At that point he stood his ground and said, "Give me back my cloak! Should I have camels to the number of these bushes I would have apportioned them amongst you, and then you shall not find me to be stingy, or deceitful or cowardly."[7]

---

4 Related Abū al-Shaykh in *Akhlāq al-Nabī ṣallallāhu ʿalayhi wassalam wa Ādābihi* (no. 92).

5 Related Abū al-Shaykh in *Akhlāq al-Nabī ṣallallāhu ʿalayhi wassalam wa Ādābihi* (no. 95).

6 Related by al-Tirmidhī in *al-Shamāʾil* (no. 355) and Abū al-Shaykh in *Akhlāq al-Nabī ṣallallāhu ʿalayhi wassalam wa Ādābihi* (no. 99).

7 Related by al-Bukhārī (no. 2821), of the ḥadīth of Jubayr ibn Muṭʿim—God be well-pleased with him.

10

An Account of His Bravery (God Bless Him and Grant Him Peace)

THE Prophet—God bless him and grant him peace—was the most valiant and courageous of people. ʿAlī—God be well-pleased with him—said, "You have surely seen me at the battle of Badr while we were taking refuge with the Prophet—God bless him and grant him peace. He was the nearest of us to the enemy and the most forceful of people that day in his intrepidity."[1] He also said, "When the pressure intensified and each party confronted the other, we defended ourselves by the Messenger of God—God bless him and grant him peace—for there was none in more proximity to the enemy than him."[2]

It was said, "The Prophet—God bless him and grant him peace—was sparse in speech and sparse in conversation. When he commanded the people to battle he would set to work briskly with thorough preparation and he would be the most intrepid of people."[3] The courageous person was the one who was close to him in battle, due to his proximity to the enemy.[4]

ʿImrān ibn Ḥuṣayn said, "The Messenger of God—God bless

1 Related by Abū al-Shaykh in *Akhlāq al-Nabī ṣallallāhu ʿalayhi wassalam wa Ādābihi* (no. 104).

2 Related by Ahmad in *al-Musnad* (1:156); and by Abū al-Shaykh in *Akhlāq al-Nabī ṣallallāhu ʿalayhi wassalam wa Ādābihi* (no. 105); and similarly by Muslim (no. 1776).

3 Related by Abū al-Shaykh in *Akhlāq al-Nabī ṣallallāhu ʿalayhi wassalam wa Ādābihi* (no. 106).

4 A similar meaning is related in Muslim (no. 1776).

him and grant him peace—did not encounter a squadron but he would be the first to commence assault upon it."[5]

And they said, "He was relentless in his valor."[6] When the polytheists pressed upon him he alighted from his mount and proceeded to say:

I am the Prophet with no falsehood;
I am the son of ʿAbd al-Muṭṭalib.

And none was seen that day who was more resolute than him.[7]

5 Related by Abū al-Shaykh in *Akhlāq al-Nabī ṣallallāhu ʿalayhi wassalam wa Ādābihi* (no. 110).

6 Related by Abū al-Shaykh in *Akhlāq al-Nabī ṣallallāhu ʿalayhi wassalam wa Ādābihi* (no. 114).

7 Related by Abū al-Shaykh in *Akhlāq al-Nabī ṣallallāhu ʿalayhi wassalam wa Ādābihi* (no. 119), and similarly by al-Bukhārī (no. 2864) and Muslim (no. 1776).

11

An Account of His Humility (God Bless Him and Grant Him Peace)

THE Prophet—God bless him and grant him peace—was the humblest of people notwithstanding his elevated status. Ibn ʿĀmir said, "I saw him throwing the *jamrah*[1] on a gray she-camel, and there was no striking, no shoving, and no (shouting) 'make way, make way.'"[2] He used to ride his donkey, to which was fastened a padded saddle that was covered with a velvety saddle-cloth, and he would have someone riding it behind him.[3] He used to visit the sick, escort the funeral bier, honor the invitations of bondsmen,[4] mend his sandals and patch his clothes. He would do the household chores with his family so as to cater to their needs.[5]

His Companions did not rise for him because of what they knew of his dislike for that.[6] He would pass by children and greet

---

1 i.e., the ritual throwing of the pebbles, symbolizing the stoning of the Devil, during the Pilgrimage (*al-Ḥajj*).

2 Related by Abū al-Shaykh in *Akhlāq al-Nabī ṣallallāhu ʿalayhi wassalam wa Ādābihi* (no. 120), al-Tirmidhī (no. 903) and Ibn Mājah (no. 3035).

3 Related by al-Bukhārī (no. 2987) and Muslim (no. 1798), of the ḥadīth of ʿUsāmah ibn Zayd—God be well-pleased with him.

4 Related by Abū al-Shaykh in *Akhlāq al-Nabī ṣallallāhu ʿalayhi wassalam wa Ādābihi* (no. 121).

5 Related by Abū al-Shaykh in *Akhlāq al-Nabī ṣallallāhu ʿalayhi wassalam wa Ādābihi* (no. 122).

6 Related by Abū al-Shaykh in *Akhlāq al-Nabī ṣallallāhu ʿalayhi wassalam wa Ādābihi* (no. 126).

them with peace. A man was brought into the presence of the Prophet—God bless him and grant him peace—and he quivered out of awe of him, whereupon he said, "Take it easy, for I am not a king. I am only the son of a woman of Quraysh who used to eat dried meat."[7]

He would sit among his Companions, mingling with them just as if he were one of them. A stranger would then come along and he would not know which among them was him until he inquired. Oftentimes this happened, so eventually they asked him to sit in a manner by which a stranger might recognize him. They thus built for him a bench of earth and he would sit on it.[8]

ʿĀʾishah—God be well-pleased with her—said, "Eat—God render me thy ransom—reclining, for it is more relaxing for you." She said further, "At which he inclined his head until his forehead almost touched the ground, and then he said, 'Rather, I eat as a slave eats, and I sit as a slave sits.'"[9] He would not eat off a raised tray[10] or use a small bowl for dipping his bread until he returned to God Most High.[11] None of his Companions would call out for him except that he would say, "At your service."[12]

When he sat with people, if they conversed about the meaning of the Afterlife he would join them in their conversation. If they talked about food or drink he would talk with them, and if they conversed about the world he would converse with them,[13] in order to be gentle and down-to-earth towards them. They would at times recite poetry in his presence and make mention of things concerning

---

7 Related by Abū al-Shaykh in *Akhlāq al-Nabī ṣallallāhu ʿalayhi wassalam wa Ādābihi* (no. 138), and similarly by Ibn Mājah (no. 3312), of the ḥadīth of Abū Masʿūd al-Anṣārī—God be well-pleased with him.

8 Related by Abū al-Shaykh in *Akhlāq al-Nabī ṣallallāhu ʿalayhi wassalam wa Ādābihi* (no. 139).

9 Related by Abū al-Shaykh in *Akhlāq al-Nabī ṣallallāhu ʿalayhi wassalam wa Ādābihi* (no. 140).

10 Or table.

11 Related by al-Bukhārī (no. 5386), and Abū al-Shaykh in *Akhlāq al-Nabī ṣallallāhu ʿalayhi wassalam wa Ādābihi* (no. 141).

12 Related by Abū al-Shaykh in *Akhlāq al-Nabī ṣallallāhu ʿalayhi wassalam wa Ādābihi* (no. 2), and similarly by al-Nasāʾī in *al-Sunan al-Kubrā* (no. 10,797).

13 Related by Abū al-Shaykh in *Akhlāq al-Nabī ṣallallāhu ʿalayhi wassalam wa Ādābihi* (no. 4).

the affairs of the Age of Ignorance, and they would laugh and he would smile when they laughed; and thus he would not be holding them back except from what was forbidden.[14]

14 Related by Muslim (no. 2322) and Abū al-Shaykh in *Akhlāq al-Nabī ṣallallāhu ʿalayhi wassalam wa Ādābihi* (no. 6).

12

An Account of His External Manner and Countenance (God Bless Him and Grant Him Peace)

THE Messenger of God—God bless him and grant him peace—with respect to the description of his physique, was neither overly tall nor excessively short.[1] Rather, he was considered to be of medium height when he walked alone. Nevertheless, God's Messenger—God bless him and grant him peace—always appeared taller than apparently tall people when they walked with him. Now and then two tall men would be flanking him and he would still appear taller than them; but when they left him, they seemed tall whereas the Prophet—blessing and peace be on him—would appear (again) to be of medium stature. The Prophet—God bless him and grant him peace—would say, "All good has been made in moderate measure."[2]

As for his complexion, the Prophet—God bless him and grant him peace—was luminous in tone (*azhar al-lawn*), and he was neither tanned nor extremely white. *Al-azhar* (luminosity) is a lucid whiteness that is unblemished with yellowness or redness or any other color. His paternal uncle, Abū Ṭālib, described him by saying:[3]

A fairness such that clouds by his countenance
are won over to send down their rain;
A sanctuary for orphans, a refuge for widows.[4]

1 i.e., his overall physique was well-proportioned; see al-Bukhārī (no. 3548) and Muslim (no. 2347).

2 Related by al-Bayhaqī in *Dalāʾil al-Nubuwwah* (1:298).

3 In *Dīwān Abū Ṭālib* (p. 75); see aslo *Iḥyāʾ*, Dār al-Fayhāʾ ed., 3:493n.1.

4 Related by al-Bukharī (no. 1009) and Ibn Mājah (no. 1272).

Some described him to be of a reddish hue, and thus they said, "Only what was exposed of him to the sun and the wind was of a reddish hue, such as his face and neck, whereas what was covered by his clothing was luminous in tone, free from any reddish tint."

The perspiration on the Prophet's face—God bless him and grant him peace—was like beads of pearls more fragrant than the most pleasant musk. As for his hair, it was wavy in a becoming manner, being neither lank nor tightly curled; and when he combed it with a comb it became like ripples in the sand. It has been said that his hair brushed against his shoulders, but most reports say that his hair reached his earlobes. Sometimes he made his hair into four plaits such that each ear would show between two plaits; and sometimes he put his hair over his ears such that the sides of his neck appeared to glow. The gray hairs on his head and beard did not exceed seventeen.

The Prophet—God bless him and grant him peace—was the most fine-looking and luminous of men. All who described him likened him to the moon on the night when it was full. His anger and his pleasure would be manifest on his face due to the limpidness of his skin. They would say, "He was as his friend Abū Bakr the Truthful—God be well-pleased with him—described him when he said:

Trustworthy, chosen one, inviting to goodness,
Like the light of the full moon dispelling darkness."[5]

The Prophet—God bless him and grant him peace—had a wide forehead and long, beautifully arched eyebrows, and there was a brightness in the space between his eyebrows like that of pure silver. His had wide, deep-black eyes, with a tinge of redness in them, and long eyelashes that almost obscured the edges of the eyelids due to their profusion. The bridge of his nose was aquiline, that is, he had a straight nose.

His teeth were evenly spaced,[6] and when he smiled they showed such that they were like a gleam of lightning when it flashes. Of God's servants, he had the finest-looking lips and the most refined closed

5 In *Dīwan Abū Bakr* (p. 36).

6 i.e., having slight interstices in between them, or in between the incisors according to some reports.

mouth. He had firm, even cheeks, and his face was neither longish nor roundish. He let his beard grow but clipped his moustache. Of God's servants, he had the finest-looking neck, which was neither long nor short; and what was exposed of it to the sun or wind was like a pitcher of silver infused with gold that glistened in both the whiteness of the silver and the redness of the gold.

The Prophet—God bless him and grant him peace—was broad of chest, like a looking glass in its evenness and the moon in its fairness, while no flesh on a part of his body folded over another part.[7] A line of hair connected between the upper part of his chest and his navel and extended like a staff, there being no other hair on his chest or abdomen. He had three creases on his abdomen, one of which was covered with his waist cloth while the other two were exposed.

He had broad, hairy shoulders, along with bulky chief bones, that is, the main bones of the shoulders, elbows and hips. He was broad of back, having the Seal of Prophethood between his two shoulder blades such that it adjoined his right shoulder. In it was a black birthmark inclining toward yellow, around which was a sequence of hairs like a horse's mane.

He had well-rounded upper arms and forearms, and his two ulnas were longish. He was broad of palms and lithe, supple of limbs, while his fingers were as wands of silver. His palms were softer than silk, and they were like the fragrant palms of a perfumer regardless of whether he applied perfume to them, such that a person would shake his hands and he would find their fragrance lingering for the remainder of the day. He would place his hand on a boy's head and the boy would stand out from among the other boys due to the fragrance lingering on his head. He was well-rounded in what was beneath the waist cloth of the thighs and shanks.

He was well-proportioned in his physique in respect of body fat, inclining somewhat towards stoutness in his later years, yet his flesh remained nearly just as firm as it was during his younger life, unaffected by body fat.[8] As regards the Prophet's manner of

7 al-Bayhaqī in *Dalāʾil al-Nubuwwah* (1:304).

8 i.e., his physique was still firm, strong and well-proportioned, without excess body fat, and unaffected by old age.

walking—God bless him and grant him peace—he walked as if he was proceeding from a stony ground and descending from a hillside, inclining forward in his steps. He would walk in a leisurely, easygoing (*huwayna*) manner without any swagger; and *huwayna* means small strides.

The Prophet—God bless him and grant him peace—used to say, "Of all men I most resemble Ādam—peace be on him—while my father, Ibrāhīm—peace be on him—most resembled me in form and character."

He used to say, "I have ten names before my Lord. I am Muḥammad, and I am Aḥmad, and I am the Effacer by whom God effaces disbelief, and I am the Last after whom there is no one,[9] and I am the Assembler after whose steps God assembles all people, and I am the Messenger of Mercy and the Messenger of Repentance and the Messenger of Battles and the Successor, for I succeeded all the Prophets, and I am Qutham."[10] Abū al-Bakhtarī said, "Al-Qutham is the perfect, the gatherer." And God knows best.

9 i.e., no prophet will come after him.

10 Related by Ibn ʿAdī in *al-Kāmil* (7:64), and similarly by Ibn ʿAsākir in *Tārīkh Dimashq* (3:28), al-Bukharī (no. 3532), and Muslim (nos. 2354, 2355).

13

An Account of His Miracles and Signs Indicative of His Truthfulness (God Bless Him and Grant Him Peace)

KNOW that whoever has witnessed the conduct of the Prophet—God bless him and grant him peace—or lent his ear to listen to the reports concerning his moral character, deeds and deportment, his habits and dispositions, and his presiding over the various groups of people, his guidance toward their rectification, his reconciliation between the various factions of people, and his leading them toward his obedience, along with what has been related of the marvels of his responses to mystifying questions and the skillfulness of his management of the well-being of people, and the excellences of his instruction in explicating the clear teachings of the Revealed Law, the grasp of whose elementary subtleties has well-nigh overwhelmed the jurists and the sages throughout their entire lifetimes, there cannot remain for him any doubt or uncertainty regarding the fact that all of this was not by way of wily acquisition through mere human capacity.

Rather, none of that is conceivable except through the procurement of heavenly succor and divine power. It is not conceivable for a liar or a deceiver. On the contrary, his comprehensive qualities of character and manners of conduct are definite testimonies to his truthfulness, so much so that when a pure, desert Arab saw him he was moved to say, "By God! This is not the face of a liar."[1] This man testified to his

1 Related by al-Tirmidhī (no. 2485) and Ibn Mājah (no. 1334).

truthfulness by virtue of the very fact of his comprehensive qualities. Therefore, how much more so is the case for someone who witnessed his moral character and experienced his manners of conduct in all of his comings and goings?

We have presented only some aspects of his moral character in order that the ethical virtues be made known, and to give notice of his truthfulness—God bless him and grant him peace—and of the loftiness of his stature and his great station with God Most High. God bestowed all of that upon him, even though he was an unlettered man who did not engage in the pursuit of the sciences or the study of books and never travelled at all in quest for knowledge, and even though he was brought up in the midst of the most notable ignorants of the Arabs as an orphan who was weak and deemed weak. Hence, from where did he obtain these excellences of character and comportment and understanding of beneficial legal knowledge, for example, quite apart from the other sciences, to say nothing of his intimate knowledge of God Most High and His angels and His books, as well as other aspects of knowledge pertaining to the specificities of Prophecy, were it not from the clarity of Revelation? How can a mere man obtain all these on his own accord? Even if he had only these manifest matters (indicative of his veracity), they would nonetheless suffice.[2]

His signs and miracles have indeed become manifest, regarding which the acquirer of knowledge cannot harbor any misgiving. We shall mention from their totality only those reports that have become widespread and are included in the authentic books[3] in order to indicate where these anthologies can be found without dwelling at length on the narration of the details therein.

More than once, God ruptured at his hands the customary course of things, as when: He split the moon for him at Makkah when the Quraysh asked him for a sign;[4] he provided food for a large group of people in the house of Jābir,[5] in the house of Abū Ṭalhah, and at the

2 I.e., sufficed as proofs of the truth and reality of his prophethood.

3 i.e., of ḥadīth and *sīrah* (prophetic biography).

4 Related by al-Bukhārī (nos. 3636, 3868) and Muslim (nos. 2800, 2802).

5 Related by al-Bukhārī (nos. 4101, 4102) and Muslim (no. 2039).

battle of the Ditch;[6] he once fed eighty[7] people from four *mudds*[8] of barley and a young she-kid (*ʿināq*), which is among the offspring of goats and older than a one-year male goat (*ʿatūd*);[9] he once fed more than eighty men from four loafs of barley bread that was carried by Anas in his hands;[10] and he once fed the army[11] from a small amount of dates that Bashīr's daughter brought in her hands, and they all ate until they were satiated from them and still there remained some surplus for them.[12]

Water sprung forth from between his fingers—blessing and peace be on him—and the whole army drank, and they were parched.[13] They did their ablutions from a small bowl even though it was too small for the Prophet—blessing and peace be on him—to stretch his hand in.[14] He—blessing and peace be on him—poured forth water for his ablution at the spring of Tabūk when there was no water in it, and did the same another time at the well of Hudaybiyah, and they both then swelled with water. The army, which numbered in the thousands, drank from the spring of Tabūk until they quenched their thirst; and one thousand five hundred drank from the well of Hudaybiyah whereas previously there had been no water in it.[15]

The Prophet—blessing and peace be on him—directed ʿUmar ibn al-Khaṭṭāb—God be well-pleased with him—to provide four hundred riders with dates. These were heaped up in the form of a camel resting with its chest on the ground, which was its kneeling pose. ʿUmar provided for all of them from that heap of dates and

---

6 Related by al-Bukhārī (no. 3578) and Muslim (no. 2040).

7 Most probably eight hundred (see *Itḥāf*, 7:167).

8 A *mudd* is a volume measure equivalent to 0.51 liters as estimated by Nuh Ha Mim Keller in *Reliance of the Traveller: A Classic Manual of Islamic Sacred Law* (Beltsville, MA: Amana, 1997), 873.

9 Related by al-Bayhaqī in *Dalāʾil al-Nubuwwah* (3:422).

10 Related by Muslim (no. 2040), of the ḥadīth of Anas.

11 Combatants at the battle of the Ditch.

12 Related by al-Bayhaqī in *Dalāʾil al-Nubuwwah* (3:427) of the ḥadīth of the daughter of Bashīr ibn Saʿīd.

13 Related by al-Bukhārī (no. 3576) and Muslim (no. 1856), of the ḥadīth of Jābir—God be well-pleased with him

14 Related by al-Bukhārī (no. 169) and Muslim (no. 2279).

15 The Tabūk miracle is related by Muslim (no. 706), of the ḥadīth of Muʿādh—God be well-pleased with him. The Hudaybiyah miracle is related by al-Bukhārī (no. 2734) and Muslim (no. 1807), and they were one thousand and four hundred.

still there remained a surplus in his custody.[16] He threw a handful of earth at the (enemy) army and their eyes were thereby blinded. The Qur'ān was revealed in regard to this incident in the statement of God Most High, "*You threw not when you threw, but God indeed threw.*"[17]

God Most High abolished the practice of divination by virtue of sending forth the Prophet—God bless him and grant him peace—and thus it disappeared, whereas previously it had been openly prevalent.[18] The tree stump from which he used to deliver his address yearned for him when the pulpit had been made for him, so much so that all his Companions heard something like the sound of a camel issuing from it. So he embraced it, whereupon it fell quiet.[19]

He challenged the Jews regarding the coveting of death while telling them that they would not be coveting it, and hence it was interposed between them and their speech and they were unable to proclaim their desire for death.[20] This incident is mentioned in the verse that is read out aloud on Friday in all the congregational mosques of the people of Islam, from the East of the Earth to the West, as an exaltation of the sign therein.[21]

The Prophet—blessing and peace be on him—was informed about unseen matters. He gave notice that ʿUthmān[22] would be overtaken by a tribulation after which he would attain to Paradise;[23] that ʿAmmār[24] would be killed by the rebellious faction;[25] and that through (his grandson) al-Ḥasan, God would bring about peace between two great

---

16 Related by Aḥmad in his *Musnad* (5:445), of the ḥadīth of al-Nuʿmān ibn Muqarrin—God be well-pleased with him.

17 Qur'ān, *al-Anfāl* (Spoils of War), 8:17; related by Muslim (no. 1777), of the ḥadīth of Salamah ibn al-Akwāʿ—God be well-pleased with him.

18 Related by al-Kharā'iṭī in *Hawātif al-Jinān* (no. 4), al-Bukhārī (no. 773), and Muslim (no. 449).

19 Related by al-Bukhārī (no. 918).

20 Related by al-Nasā'ī in *al-Sunan al-Kubrā* (no. 10, 995), of the ḥadīth of Ibn ʿAbbās—God be well-pleased with him.

21 *al-Jumuʿah*, 62:6-8.

22 i.e., ʿUthmān ibn ʿAffān, the second caliph of Islām—God be well-pleased with him.

23 Related by al-Bukhārī (no. 3674), and Muslim (no. 2403).

24 ʿAmmār ibn Yāsir—God be well-pleased with him—who was killed fighting on the side of ʿAlī—God be well-pleased with him—at the battle of Ṣiffīn.

25 That is, he committed suicide; related by al-Bukhārī (no. 447), and Muslim (no. 2915).

factions of the Muslims.[26] He—blessings and peace be on him—spoke of a man who was fighting in the path of God, saying that he would be of the people of the Fire, and such became evident because (it later turned out that) the man had killed himself.[27]

Now, all these are matters that can never be known by any of the various ways of acquiring knowledge: not by way of the stars[28] or armomancy (*katif*),[29] nor by way of drawing lines (*khaṭṭ*)[30] or augury (*zajr*).[31] They can only be known by God Most High informing and revealing them to him.

Surāqah (ibn Mālik) ibn Juʿsham pursued him but the hoofs of his horse sank into the earth and the dust overwhelmed him, so much so that he had to call out to him for help, whereupon he prayed for him and thus his horse broke free. He then gave notice to him that soon he would be wearing the bracelets of Chosroes on his forearms,[32] and so it came to pass.[33]

He reported the killing of al-Aswad al-ʿAnsī the Liar on the night he was killed, whereas the man was in Sanʿāʾ in Yemen, and he also reported the person who killed him.[34] He confronted one hundred of the Quraysh who were lying in wait for him and cast some earth over their heads and thus they failed to see him.[35] A male camel made a complaint to him and abased itself before him.[36] He said to a group of his Companions who were gathered, "One of you is in the

---

26 Related by al-Bukhārī (no. 2704); the two factions allude to the party of ʿAlī and the the party of Muʿāwiyah—God be well-pleased with them—and peace between the two was brought about when, after the matyrdom of ʿAlī, Ḥasan—God be well-pleased with him—relinquished his right to the Caliphate.

27 Related by al-Bukhārī (no. 2898), and Muslim (no. 112).

28 I.e., astrology.

29 I.e., divination by way of inspecting the shoulder blade of an animal.

30 I.e., a method of geomancy by drawing lines in the sand.

31 I.e., augury or ornithomancy, a form of divination by observing the flight of birds to the left or right.

32 i.e., Khosrow II, or Khusraw Parvez, the last great king of the Sassanian Empire, who reigned from 590-628 CE.

33 Related by al-Bukhārī (no. 3615), Muslim (no. 2009) and al-Bayhaqī in *Dalāʾil al-Nubuwwah* (6:325).

34 Related by al-Bukhārī (no. 4375) and Muslim (no. 2273).

35 Related by al-Ṭabarī in his *Tārīkh* (2:372) and documented by ibn Ḥazm in *Jawāmiʿ al-Sīrah* (p. 11).

36 Related by Abū Dāwūd (no. 2549) and Aḥmad in *al-Musnad* (3:158).

Fire; its molar tooth is as (big as) Uḥud." Thereafter, they all died in the constancy of faith except one of them, who apostatized and was killed as an apostate.[37] He told another group of his Companions, "The last of you to die will be in the fire," and so the last of them fell lifeless into the fire where he was immolated and died."[38] He called out to two trees and they came to him and joined together; then he directed them away and they separated.[39]

The Prophet—God bless him and grant him peace—was of medium stature but when he walked with tall people he was taller than them.

He—blessing and peace be on him—urged the Christians to mutual imprecation (*mubāhalah*)[40] but they declined; and the Prophet—God bless him and grant him peace—informed them that had they done so, they would have perished; and thus they knew the soundness of his statement and declined to imprecate.[41]

ʿĀmir ibn al-Ṭufayl ibn Mālik and Arbad ibn Qays, who were horsemen and assassins of the Arabs, came to the Prophet—blessing and peace be on him—with the intent of killing him, but something intervened between them and their intended deed, whereupon he prayed against them; and consequently Amir perished by a plague, whereas Arbad perished by lightning that immolated him.[42]

The Prophet—blessings and peace be on him—foretold that he would kill Ubayy ibn Khalaf al-Jumaḥī, and thus it came to pass that he scratched him slightly at the battle of Uḥud, and therein was his fate of death.[43]

The Prophet—blessings and peace be on him—was fed a poisoned

37 Related by al-Ṭabarānī in *al-Kabīr* (3:283); see also *Jawāmiʿ al-Sīrah* (p. 11).

38 Related by al-Dulābī in *al-Kunyā waʾl-Asmāʾ* (1:115), and al-Bayhaqī in *Dalāʾil al-Nubuwwah* (6:458).

39 Related by Muslim (no. 3012), of the ḥadīth of Jābir—God be well-pleased with him.

40 i.e., prayer to withdraw mercy from whoever lies or engages in falsehood.

41 Related by al-Nasāʾī in *al-Sunan al-Kubrā* (no. 10,995), of the ḥadīth of Ibn Abbās—God be well-pleased with him; incident alluded to in the Qurʾān, *Āl ʿImrān* (Family of ʿImrān), 3:61.

42 Related by al-Ṭabarāni in *al-Awsaṭ* (no. 9123), of the ḥadīth of Ibn Abbās—God be well-pleased with them both and similarly by Aḥmad in his *Musnad* (3:210), of the ḥadīth of Anas—God be well-pleased with him.

43 Related by Ibn Saʿd in his *Ṭabaqāt* (2:43), and al-Bayhaqī in *Dalāʾil al-Nubuwwah* (3:211).

dish, and while the one who ate it with him died, he—God bless him and grant him peace—lived thereafter for four more years; and that poisoned arm (of mutton) spoke to him.[44]

At the Battle of Badr, the Prophet—blessings and peace be on him—foretold the locations in which the notables of the Quraysh would be slain, and he assigned for them, one man after another, their respective locations such that not a single one of them strayed away from his designated spot.[45]

He—blessing and peace be on him—foretold that some parties of his Community would engage in military expeditions at sea, and so it came to pass.[46] The Earth was folded up for him such that its western and eastern regions were shown to him, and he foretold that a king of his Community would reach those regions that were folded up for him, and thus it came to pass. A king of his Community did indeed reach the near regions of the East and parts of the countries of the Turks, and the far regions of the West, including the sea of Andalusia and the lands of the Berbers; but they did not expand to the South or to the North,[47] precisely as he—God bless him and grant him peace—had indicated.[48]

He foretold that his daughter, Fāṭimah—God be well-pleased with her—would be the first of his family to meet him (in the Afterlife), and so it came to pass.[49] He informed his womenfolk that she whose hands were longest would be the soonest of them to meet him, and it so happened that Zaynab bint Jaḥsh al-Asadiyyah—God be well-pleased with her—was the most long-handed of them in respect of alms-giving and thus she became the soonest of them to meet him.[50]

He stroked the udder of a barren ewe that was not giving milk and she soon flowed with milk, and that was the cause of Ibn Masʿūd—God

---

44 i.e., saying that it was poisoned; related by Abū Dāwūd (no. 4510), al-Bukhārī (no. 2617), and Muslim (no. 2190).

45 Related by Muslim (no. 2873).

46 Related by al-Bukhārī (no. 2789) and Muslim (no. 1912).

47 i.e., not to the far North or far South.

48 Related by Muslim (no. 2889).

49 Related by al-Bukhārī (no. 3624) and Muslim (no. 2450).

50 Related by Muslim (no. 2452), of the ḥadīth of ʿĀʾishah—God be well-pleased with her.

be well-pleased with him—becoming Muslim.[51] He did that another time in the tent of Umm Maᶜbad al-Khuzāᶜiyyah. The eye of one of his Companions became dislodged and fell out, and he—blessing and peace be on him—put it back with his hand, and it became the sounder and finer of his two eyes.[52] He spat into the eye of ᶜAlī—God be well-pleased with him—after it had become sore at the Battle of Khaybar and it became well immediately, whereupon he assigned him the banner.[53] They used to hear the food glorifying God in his presence—God bless him and grant him peace.[54] The foot of one of the Companions of the Prophet—God bless him and grant him peace—was smitten with a disease, but he rubbed it with his hand and it recovered at once.[55]

The provisions of the army that was following him—blessings and peace be on him—had diminished and so he called for everything that was still remaining, but only a very small amount was collected. He then prayed that it be blessed and directed them to partake of it, and thus it came to pass that not a single vessel remained in the army camp but that it became filled with provisions.[56]

Al-Ḥakam ibn Abī al-ᶜĀs mimicked the gait of the Prophet—blessings and peace be on him—in a derisive manner, whereupon the Prophet—blessing and peace be on him—said, "Be like that," and thus he never ceased trembling until he died.[57] The Prophet—blessing and peace be on him—proposed to a woman, but her father said to him, "Verily she is afflicted with leprosy," as an excuse to decline his proposal, even though she was not leprous, whereupon he—blessings and peace be on him—said, "Let her then be so," and thus she became leprous; and she was the mother of the poet, Shabīb ibn al-Barṣāʾ.[58]

---

51 Related by Aḥmad in *al-Musnad* (1:462), of the ḥadīth of ᶜAbdullāh ibn Masᶜūd—God be well-pleased with him.

52 Related by Ibn Saᶜd in his *Ṭabaqāt* (1:158), and al-Bayhaqī in *Dalāʾil al-Nubuwwah* (3:251).

53 Related by al-Bukhārī (no. 2942) and Muslim (no. 2404).

54 Related by al-Bukhārī (no. 3579).

55 Related by al-Bukhārī (no. 4039); and he was ᶜAbdullāh ibn ᶜAtīk—God be well-pleased with him.

56 Related by Muslim (no. 27).

57 Related by al-Bayhaqī in *Dalāʾil al-Nubuwwah* (6:239-240), and similarly by Abū Nuᶜāym in *Maᶜrifat al-Ṣaḥābah* (2:712).

58 Related by Abū Nuᶜāym in *Maᶜrifat al-Ṣaḥābah* (6:3242).

And there are many other signs and miracles of the Prophet—God bless him and grant him peace—but we have confined ourselves to those reports that are widely known.

Whosoever casts doubt regarding the rupture of the customary course of events at his hands by supposing that each of these incidents was not successively reported by numerous narrators but that only the Qurʾān was successively transmitted, is like the one who harbors misgivings about the courage of ʿAlī—God be pleased with him—or the generosity of Ḥātim al-Ṭaʾī. It is known that such singular incidents were not successively reported by numerous sources, but nonetheless, the totality of the transmitted reports of these events does convey certain knowledge.[59]

Furthermore, the independent consecutive transmission of the Qurʾān is not doubted, for it is the greatest miracle that is everlasting amongst humankind and there is no prophet having an everlasting miracle except for him—God bless him and grant him peace. With the Qurʾān, God's Messenger—God bless him and grant him peace—challenged the people of rhetoric and the eloquent of the Arabs at a time when the Arabian Peninsular was populated with thousands of those whose vocation was the art of eloquent speech, in which they would hold contests among themselves and boast to one another.

He used to challenge the most notable of them to bring forth its resemblance, or ten chapters like it, or even just one chapter like it, should they harbor misgivings concerning it, while saying to them, "*Say, indeed if humankind and the Jinn should come together to bring forth a resemblance of this Qurʾān, they would not bring forth its likeness even if they were to aid one another*."[60] He said that to incapacitate them and thus they were incapable of bringing forth its likeness and they turned away from doing so, so much so that (by thus turning away) they exposed themselves to slaughter and their wives and children to captivity.[61] They were neither able to contend with nor censure the purity and beauty of its expression. After his time, this

59 Unlike the Qurʾān which was transmitted by numerous successive narrators (*mutawātir*), these Prophetic miracles were reported by singular narrators (*āḥād*). However, taken as a whole, these singular reports reinforce one another and thus convey certain knowledge, even if individually they convey only probable knowledge.

60 *Al-Isrāʾ* (Night Journey), 17:88.

61 i.e., when, because of their unbelief they fought against Islam, and were vanquished.

miracle of the Qurʾān spread throughout the regions of the world in the East and West, generation after generation, epoch after epoch, and today close to five hundred years have elapsed[62] and yet none have been able to match it.

Hence, how great indeed is the foolishness of those who have looked into his conduct, then his sayings, deeds, character, miracles, then the preservation of his law until the present time and its diffusion throughout the regions of the world and the compliance of the kings of the Earth with it—during his lifetime and afterwards in spite of his weakness and being an orphan—and yet have persisted thereafter in harboring misgivings regarding his truthfulness. And how great indeed is the success of those who have believed in him, affirmed his truthfulness and followed him in all matters.

We beseech God Most High to grant us ease in emulating him in his character, deeds, conduct and sayings, through His bestowal and ample munificence, for He is indeed Most Hearing, Most Near.

***

The Book of
Prophetic Ethics and the Courtesies of Living,
which is the End of the Quarter of the Norms of Daily Life of the
Book of the Revivification of the Sciences of Religion, is thus
Concluded, with Praise to God and by the refinement of His
Facilitation.
And Blessing and Peace be on the best of His creation,
Muḥammad, and on his Family and Companions.
And there follows it the Quarter of the Causes of Perdition,
which is the Third Quarter of the
Book of the Revivification of the Sciences of Religion.

62 i.e., up to the time of al-Ghazālī.

Bibliography[1]

Works in Arabic

al-Ābī, Manṣūr ibn al-Ḥusayn (d. 421 AH). *Nathr al-Durr*. Edited by Muḥammad ʿAlī Qarnah et al. Cairo: al-Hayʾat al-Miṣriyyat al-ʿĀmmah liʾl-Kuttāb, 1984.

Abū Bakr al-Shāfiʿī, Muḥammad ibn ʿAbdillāh ibn Ibrāhīm al-Bazzāz (d. 354 AH). *al-Ghaylāniyyāt*. Edited by Ḥilmī Kāmil ʿAbd al-Hādī. Ḍammām: Dār ibn al-Jawzī, n.d.

Abū Bakr Al-Ṣiddīq (d. 13 AH). *Dīwan Abū Bakr*. Edited by Rājī al-Asmar. Beirut: Dār al-Ṣādir, 2003.

Abū Dāwūd, Sulaymān b. al-Ashʿath al-Sijistānī (d. 275 AH). *Sunan Abū Dāwūd*. Edited by ʿIzzat ʿUbayd al-Daʿās and ʿĀdil al-Sayyid. Beirut: Dār Ibn Ḥazm, 1997.

Abū Nuʿaym al-Iṣbahānī, Aḥmad b. ʿAbdallāh (d. 430 AH). *Ḥilyat al-Awliyāʾ*. Cairo: Maṭbaʿāt al-Saʿādah waʾl-Khānijī, 1357 AH; Beirut: Dār al-Kitāb al-ʿArabī, 1987.

———. *Tārīkh Iṣbahān*. Edited by Sayyid Kusrawī Ḥasan. Beirut: Dār al-Kutub al-ʿIlmiyyah, 1990.

———. *Maʿrifat al-Ṣaḥābah*. Edited by ʿĀdil Yūsuf al-ʿAzzāzī. Dār al-Waṭan, 1998.

Abū al-Shaykh, ʿAbdullāh ibn Muḥammad ibn Ḥayyān (d. 369 AH). *Akhlāq al-Nabiyy ṣallallāhu ʿalayhi wassalam wa Ādābih*. Edited by Muḥammad al-Iskandarī. Beirut: Dār al-Kitāb al-ʿArabī, 2007.

Abū Ṭāhir al-Silafī, Aḥmad b. Muḥammad (d. 576 AH). *Muʿjam al-Safar*. Edited by ʿAbdullāh ʿUmar al-Bārūdī. Beirut: Dār al-Fikr, 1993.

1 Bibliography of cited works only; Arabic works cited are based for the most part on the bibliography given in the Dār al-Minhāj edition of the *Iḥyāʾ*.

Abū Ṭālib, ibn ʿAbd al-Muṭṭalib (d. 03 BH). *Dīwan Abī Ṭālib*. Edited by Muḥammad Ḥasan Āl Yāsin. Beirut: Maktabat al-Hilāl, 2009.

Abū Yaʿlā, Aḥmad b. ʿAlī al-Tamīmī al-Mawṣūlī (d. 307 AH). *Musnad Abū Yaʿlā al-Mawṣūlī*. Edited by Ḥusayn Salīm Asad al-Dārānī. Damascus: Dār al-Maʾmūn liʾl-Turāth and Dār al-Thaqāfat al-ʿArabiyyah, 1989.

Aḥmad b. Ḥanbal (d. 241 AH). *Musnad al-Imām Aḥmad b. Ḥanbal*. Edited by Shuʿayb al-Arnāʾūṭ. Beirut: Muʾassasat al-Risālah, 1995.

al-Balādhurī, Aḥmad b. Yaḥyā (d. 279 AH). *Ansāb al-Ashrāf*. Edited by Suhayb Zakkār and Riyāḍ Zarkalī. Beirut: Dār al-Fikr, 1996.

al-Bayhaqī, Aḥmad b. al-Ḥusayn (d. 458 AH). *al-Sunan al-Kubrā*. Edited by al-Sayyid Hāshim al-Nadwī. Hyderabad, 1356 AH (repr. Beirut: Dār al-Maʿrifah, n.d.).

———. *al-Zuhd al-Kabīr*. Edited by ʿĀmir Aḥmad Ḥaydar. Beirut: Muʾassasat al-Kutub al-Thaqāfiyyah, 1996.

———. *Dalāʾil al-Nubuwwah wa Maʿrifat Aḥwāl Ṣāḥib al-Sharīʿah*. Edited by ʿAbd al-Muʿṭī Qalʿajī. Cairo: Dār al-Rayyān, 1988.

———. *Shuʿab al-Īmān*. Edited by Muḥammad al-Saʿīd b. Bayūnī Zaghlūl. Beirut: Dār al-Kutub al-ʿIlmiyyyah, 2000.

al-Bukhārī, Muḥammad b. Ismāʿīl (d. 256 AH). *al-Adab al-Mufrad*. Edited by Muḥammad Fūʾād ʿAbd al-Bāqī. Cairo: al-Maktab al-Salafiyyah, 1997.

———. *Ṣaḥīḥ al-Bukhārī*. Istanbul: n.p. (reprint of Beirut: Dār Ṭūq al-Najāt, 1422).

al-Dārimī, ʿAbdullāh ibn ʿAbd al-Raḥmān (d. 255 AH). *Sunan al-Dārimī* (*Musnad al-Dārimī*). Edited by Ḥusayn Salīm Asad al-Dārānī. Dār al-Mughnī, 2000.

al-Dāruquṭnī, ʿAlī ibn ʿUmar (d. 385 AH). *al-Sunan*. Edited by ʿAbdullāh Hāshim Yamāni. Beirut: Dār al-Maʿrifah, 1966.

al-Dūlābī, Muḥammad ibn Aḥmad ibn Muslim (d. 310 AH). *al-Kunā waʾl-Asmāʾ*. Hyderabad, 1322 AH.

al-Ghazālī, Muḥammad ibn Muḥammad (d. 505 AH). *Iḥyāʾ ʿUlūm al-Dīn*. Edited by ʿAlī Muḥammad Muṣṭafā and Saʿīd al-Maḥāsinī. Damascus: Dār al-Fayḥāʾ, 2010.

———. *Iḥyāʾ ʿUlūm al-Dīn*. Jeddah: Dār al-Minhāj, 2011.

al-Ḥākim al-Nīsābūrī, Muḥammad b. ʿAbdallāh (d. 403 AH). *al-Mustadrak ʿalā al-Ṣaḥiḥayn*. Hyderabad: Dāʾirat al-Maʿārif al-Niẓāmiyyah, 1335 AH (repr. Beirut: Dār al-Maʿrifah, n.d.).

al-Ḥakīm al-Tirmidhī, Muḥammad b. ʿAlī (d. 318 AH). *Nawādir al-Uṣūl fī Maʿrifat Aḥādīth al-Rasūl ṣallallāhu ʿalayhi wassalam*. Beirut: Dār Ṣādir, n.d. (reprint Cairo, 1293 edition).

Ḥannād, Ḥannād ibn al-Sariy ibn Muṣʿab al-Dārimī al-Kūfī (d. 281 AH). *al-Zuhd*. Damascus: Dār ibn Kathīr, 1999; Kuwait: Dār al-Khulafāʾ, 1406 AH.

Ibn Abī al-Dunyā, ʿAbdullāh ibn Muḥammad al-Qurashī (d. 281 AH).

Ṣifat al-Jannah wa mā Aʿadda Allāh li Ahlihā min al-Naʿīm. Edited by ʿAmr ibn ʿAbd al-Munʿim Salīm. Cairo: Maktabat ibn Taymiyyah, 1997.

———. *al-Ṣumt wa Ādāb al-Lisān*. Edited by Najm al-Dīn ʿAbd al-Raḥmān Khalaf. Beirut: Dār al-Gharb al-Islāmī, 1986.

Ibn ʿAdī, ʿAbdullāh ibn ʿAdī al-Jurjānī (d. 365 AH). *al-Kāmil fī Ḍuʿafāʾ al-Rijāl*. Suhayl Zakkār and Mukhtār Ghazāwī. Dār al-Fikr, 1988.

Ibn al-Aʿrābī, Aḥmad ibn Muḥammad ibn Bishr al-Baṣrī (d. 340 AH). *al-Muʿjam*. ʿAbd al-Muḥsin ibn Ibrāhīm al-Ḥusaynī. Dammām: Dār Ibn al-Jawzī, 1997.

Ibn ʿAsākir, ʿAlī b. al-Ḥasan (d. 571 AH). *Tārīkh Madīnat Dimashq*. Edited by Muḥibb al-Dīn ʿUmar b. Gharāmat al-ʿUmrāwī. Beirut: Dār al-Fikr, 1995.

Ibn Ḥazm, ʿAlī ibn Aḥmad ibn Saʿīd al-Ẓāhirī (d. 456 AH). *Jawāmiʿ al-Sīrah al-Nabawiyyah*. Beirut: Dār al-Kutub al-ʿIlmiyyah, 1983.

Ibn Ḥibbān, Abū Ḥātim Muḥammad (d. 354 AH). *Ṣaḥīḥ ibn Hibbān*. Dār al-Maʿārif, 1952.

Ibn Khuzaymah, Muḥammad ibn Isḥāq (d. 311 AH). *Ṣaḥīḥ ibn Khuzaymah*. Edited by Muṣṭafā al-Aʿẓāmī. al-Maktab al-Islāmī, 1980.

Ibn Mājah, Muḥammad b. Yazīd (d. 273 AH). *Sunan Ibn Mājah*. Edited by Muḥammad Fuʾād ʿAbd al-Bāqī. Cairo: Dār Iḥyāʾ al-Kutub al-ʿArabiyyah, 1954.

Ibn al-Mubārak, ʿAbdullāh (d. 191 AH). *al-Zuhd waʾl-Raqāʾiq*. Edited by Ḥabīb al-Raḥmān al-ʿAẓamī. Beirut: Dār al-Kutub al-ʿIlmiyyah, n.d.

Ibn Saʿd, Muḥammad b. Saʿd al-Baṣrī (d. 230 AH). *Kitāb al-Ṭabaqāt al-Kabīr*. Edited by ʿAlī Muḥammad ʿUmar. Cairo: Maktabat al-Khānijī, 2001.

Ibn Ṭāhir, Muḥammad al-Maqdisī (d. 507 AH). *Ṣafwat al-Taṣawwuf*. Edited by Ghādat al-Muqaddim ʿUdrah. Beirut: Dār al-Muntakhab al-ʿArabī, 1995.

Ibn Usāmah, al-Ḥārith (d. 282 AH). *Zawāʾid Musnad al-Ḥārith*, in Nūr al-Dīn ʿAlī ibn Abū Bakr al-Haythamī. *Bughyat al-Bāḥith ʿan Zawāʾid Musnad al-Ḥārith*. (Madīnah: Islamic University, 1992).

Ibn Wahb, ʿAbdullāh ibn Wahb al-Qurashī (d. 197 AH). *al-Jāmiʿ fī al-Ḥadīth*. Edited by Muṣṭafā Ḥasan Abū al-Khayr. Ḍammām: Dār ibn al-Jawzī, 1996.

al-ʿIrāqī, Zayn al-Dīn Abū Faḍl ʿAbd al-Raḥīm ibn al-Ḥusayn (d. 806 AH). *al-Mughnī ʿan al-Asfār fī al-Asfār fī Takhrīj mā fī al-Iḥyāʾ min al-Akhbār*. Cairo: Dar al-Hadith, 1992.

al-Jurjāni, Abū al-Qāsim Ḥamzah ibn Yūsuf (d. 345 AH). *Tārikh Jurjān*. Muḥammad ʿAbd al-Muʿīn Khān. Beirut: ʿAlam al-Kutub, 1980.

al-Kharāʾiṭī, Muḥammad ibn Jaʿfar (d. 327 AH). *Masāwiʾ al-Akhlāq wa Ṭarāʾiq Makrūhuhā*. Edited by Muṣṭafā ʿAṭā. Beirut: Muʾassasat al-Kutub al-Thaqāfiyyah, *1993*.

———. *Makārim al-Akhlāq*. Beirut: Dār al-Fikr, n.d.

———. *Hawātif al-Jinān*. Edited by Ibrāhīm Ṣāliḥ. Damascus: Dār al-Bashāʾir, 2001.

al-Khaṭīb al-Baghdādī, Aḥmad b. ʿAlī (d. 463 AH). *Tārīkh Baghdād*. Edited by Muṣṭafā ʿAbd al-Qādir ʿAṭā. Beirut: Dār al-Kutub al-ʿIlmiyyah, 1997.

al-Laḥji, ʿAbd ibn Saʿīd ibn Muḥammad ʿAbbādī (d. 1410 AH). *Muntahā al-Sūl*. Edited by ʿAbd al-Jalīl al-ʿAṭā al-Bakrī. Jeddah: Dār al-Minhāj, 2008.

Muslim b. al-Ḥajjāj al-Qushayrī al-Nīsābūrī (d. 261 AH). *Ṣaḥīḥ Muslim*. Edited by Muḥammad Fuʾād ʿAbd al-Bāqī. Cairo: Dār Iḥyāʾ al-Kutub al-ʿArabiyyah, 1954.

al-Nasāʾī, Abū ʿAbd al-Raḥmān Aḥmad b. Shuʿayb (d. 303 AH). *al-Sunan al-Kubrā*. Edited by Markaz al-Buḥūth wa-Taqnīyah. Cairo: Dār al-Taʾṣīl, 2012.

———. *Sunan al-Nasāʾī*. Beirut: Dār al-Kitāb al-ʿArabī, n.d.; reprint of al-Maṭbaʿat al-Maymāniyyah ed., 1312 AH.

———. *ʿAmal al-Yawm waʾl-Laylah*. Beirut: Muʾassasat al-Kutub al-Thaqāfiyyah, 1988.

al-Ṣanʿānī, ʿAbd al-Razzāq b. Hammām (d. 211 AH). *al-Muṣannaf*. Edited by Ḥabīb al-Raḥmān al-Aʿẓāmī. Cairo: Beirut: al-Majlis al-ʿIlmī and al-Maktab al-Islāmī, 1983.

al-Silafī, Abū Ṭāhir Aḥmad b. Muḥammad (d. 576 AH). *Muʿjam al-Safar*. Edited by ʿAbdullāh ʿUmar al-Bārūdī. Beirut: Dār al-Fikr, 1993.

al-Suyūṭī, ʿAbd al-Rahman ibn Abū Bakr (d. 911 AH). *al-Shamāʾil al-Sharīfah*. Edited by Ḥusayn ibn ʿUbayd Bā Hubayshī. Cairo: Dār Ṭāʾir al-ʿIlm, n.d.

al-Ṭabarānī, Sulaymān b. Aḥmad (d. 360 AH). *al-Muʿjam al-Awsaṭ*. Edited by Maḥmūd al-Ṭaḥḥān. Riyadh [?]: Maktabat al-Maʿārif, 1985.

———. *al-Muʿjam al-Kabīr*. Edited by Ḥamdī ʿAbd al-Majīd al-Salafī. Beirut: Dār Iḥyāʾ al-Turāth al-ʿArabī, n.d.

———. *Makārim al-Akhlāq*. Beirut: Dār al-Mashārīʿ, 2007.

al-Ṭabarī, Muḥammad ibn Jarīr (d. 315 AH). *Tārīkh al-Umam waʾl-Mulūk*. Edited by Muḥammad Abū al-Faḍl Ibrāhīm. Beirut: n.p., 1967.

al-Tirmidhī, Muḥammad b. ʿĪsā. (d. 279 AH). *Sunan al-Tirmidhī (al-Jāmiʿ al-Ṣaḥīḥ)*. Edited by Aḥmad Shākir, Muḥammad Fuʾād ʿAbd al-Bāqī, and Ibrāhīm ʿAṭwa. Beirut: Dār Iḥyāʾ al-Turāth al-ʿArabī, n.d. (reprint of Cairo, 1938 edition).

———. *al-Shamāʾil al-Muhammadiyyah*. Edited by Muḥammad al-ʿAwwāmah. Beirut: self-published, 2001.

al-Zabīdī, Muḥammad Murtaḍā (d. 1205 AH). *Itḥāf al-Sadāt al-Muttaqīn bi Sharḥ Iḥyāʾ ʿUlūm al-Dīn*. Beirut: Dār Iḥyāʾ al-Turāth al-ʿArabī, 1994.

Works in English

al-Attas, Syed Muhammad Naquib, *Islam and Secularism*, 2nd imprint. Kuala Lumpur: ISTAC, 1993.

———. *Prolegomena to the Metaphysics of Islam: An Exposition of the Fundamental Elements of the Worldview of Islam*. Kuala Lumpur: ISTAC, 2001.

Bewley, Aisha Abdarrahman, trans. al-Qāḍī ʿIyāḍ. *Muhammad, Messenger of God*, rev. ed. Norwich: Diwan Press, 2011.

Cleary, Thomas. *The Quran: A New Translation*. Starlatch, 2006.

Hamidullah, Muhammad. *Le Prophete del' Islam: Sa Vie et Son Ouevre* (1959). Trans. Mahmood Ahmad Ghazi, *The Life and Work of the Prophet of Islam*. Islamabad: Islamic Research Institute, 1998.

Keller, Nūḥ Hā Mīm. *Reliance of the Traveller: A Classic Manual of Islamic Sacred Law.* Translation of Aḥmad ibn Nāqib al-Miṣrī's *ʿUmdat al-Sālik*. Evanston, IL: Sunna Books, 1993.

Holland, Muhtar, trans., *A Portrait of the Prophet as Seen by His Contemporaries* (Fons Vitae, 2014).

Lane, Edward William and Stanley Lane-Pool. *Arabic-English Lexicon*. 2 vols. Cambridge: Islamic Texts Society, 1984.

Pickthall, Muhammad Marmaduke. *The Glorious Qurʾan: Text and Explanatory Translation*. Mecca: Muslim World League, 1977.

Roberts, Nancy, trans. Saʿīd Ramaḍān al-Būṭī. *Jurisprudence of the Prophetic Biography* Damascus: Dar al-Fikr,.

Wehr, Hans. *A Dictionary of Modern Written Arabic*. Urbana, IL: Spoken Language Services, 1994.

Zolondek, Leon. Trans. *Book XX of al-Ghazali's Iḥyāʾ ʿUlūm al-Dīn*. Leiden: Brill, 1963.

Index of Qurʾānic Verses

3:6 166
3:128 9
3:134 8
3:159 24
5:13 8
7:199 8
8:17 64
16:90 8, 11
17:88 69
24:22 8
31:17 8
40:60 7
41:34 8
42:43 8
49:12 8
62:6-8 64
68:4 9

Index of *Ḥadīth*

A Bedouin came to him one day while he…, 29
A fairness, such that clouds by his countenance are won over to send down their rain; A sanctuary for orphans, a refuge for widows, 57
Accept Islam, for Muḥammad gives as the giving of one who harbors no fear of want, 49
ʿAlī comes to you in the Cloud!, 39
All good has been made in moderate measure, 57
All praise be to God Who has dressed me with that by which I conceal my nakedness and by which I adorn myself amongst people, 40
At your service, 54

Be like that, 68
By God! This is not the face of a liar, 61
By Him who sent him with the Truth, he never once said to me about something he disliked, 'Why did you do that?', 22
By the One in Whose grip is my soul, none enters the Garden but those of good character, 10

Clothe your living in them, and shroud your dead in them, 37

Do not allow a part of the Qurʾān to contradict another, for it has been revealed in various aspects, 28
"Do you have a need?" When the person's need was satisfied he returned to his prayer, 23
Draw people close and do not drive them away, 47

The ethical character of God's Messenger—God bless him and grant him peace—is the Qurʾān, 7-8

Give me back my cloak! Should I have camels to the number of these bushes I would have apportioned them amongst you, and then you shall not find me to be niggardly, or deceitful or cowardly…, 50
Go until you come to Rawḍat Khākh, for a woman in a howdah is there with a letter; take it from her…, 45
God did not empower you to do so, 44
God have mercy on my brother Mūsā, for he was hurt by more than this and yet he showed patience, 46

Have I done good to you?..., 47
He—God bless him and grant him peace—never complained about his bedding…, 22
He did not converse in his speech the way you do; his speech was laconic while you render yours so prosaic, 27
He did not leave aside a good counsel or a fine disposition except that he would call us toward it and command us to realize it, 11
He was among the most smiling of people and the most pleasant of them in personality…, 29
He was the most concise of people in speech, for Jibrīl came to him in that manner of speech…, 27
He was the most munificent of all people, the most open-hearted, the most truthful in speech…, 49
He was relentless in his valor, 52
How shall a people be successful who stain the face of their Prophet with blood even as he calls them to their Lord?, 8

I am only a slave, I dress as the slave dresses, 38
I am the most eloquent of the Arabs, 27
I am the Prophet with no falsehood; I am the son of ʿAbd al-Muṭṭalib, 52
I do not forbid it, but I detest vanity and facing the reckoning for the excesses of the world on the morrow; and I desire humility, for indeed, whoever is humble before God, God will exalt him, 36
I have been sent to perfect the nobilities of ethical character, 9
I have come back to you from the presence of the best of men, 44
I have not seen his likeness—God bless him and grant him peace—neither before nor after him…, 49
I have ten names before my Lord. I am Muḥammad, and I am Aḥmad, and I am the Effacer by whom God effaces disbelief, and I am the Last after whom there is no one, and I am the Assembler upon whose step God assembles all people, and I am the Messenger of Mercy and the Messenger of Repentance and the Messenger of Battles and the Successor, for I succeeded all the Prophets, and I am Qutham, 60
I saw him throwing the *jamrah* on a gray she-camel, and there was no striking, no shoving, and no (shouting) 'make way, make way', 53
I seek refuge in God that people should say that I kill my Companions, 44

I was only sent as a mercy, and I was not sent as a curser, 21
If only you had told him to desist from it, 47
In the name of God; O God! Make this a blessing for which gratitude is shown, and through which is attained the blessing of the Garden, 31
Indeed, the likeness of me and this Bedouin is as the likeness of a man who had a she-camel which ran away from him…, 48
Indeed, it has no blessing, for God did not feed us fire, so cool it, 31
Indeed, it is not known on which fingers the blessing is, 35
It improves the sense of hearing; and it is the chief of foods in this world and the Hereafter…, 33
It is of the Garden, and a cure for poison and sorcery, 34
It is *sunnah* (preferred custom) to give it to you, but if you wish you may prefer them (over yourself), 35
It is the tree of my brother, Yūnus—peace be on him, 33

Jibrīl—on whom be peace—has taught me these words, 25

The last of you to die will be in the fire," and so the last of them fell lifeless into the fire where he was immolated and died, 66
The last morsel of the food contains the most blessing, 35
Leave him alone, for this is already written and preordained, 22
Let none of you convey to me anything regarding any one of my Companions, for I would like to go out to you with a sound heart, 46
Let you free her, for his father used to love the nobilities of ethical character, and God verily loves the nobilities of character, 10

The Messenger of God—God bless him and grant him peace—did not encounter a squadron but he would be the first to commence assault upon it, 51
Muḥammad is the Messenger of God, My chosen servant. He is not coarse…, 22
My father and mother be your ransom! What has become of the black garment?..., 39

O ʿĀʾishah, when you cook in the pot put in plenty of gourds, for it fortifies the heart of the distressed, 33
O God, beautify my physical form and my ethical character, 7
O God! Be Thou sanctified and praised; I bear witness that there is no god but Thou…, 25
O God, make me shun wicked character traits, 7
O God! Show me the truth as truth that I might follow it…, 30
O Muʿādh! I enjoin upon you to be mindful of God, to be truthful in speech, to fulfill agreements, to honor trusts…, 11
O my Lord! For You is the praise; You fed and thus You sated; and You gave drink and thus You quenched. For You is the praise undenied, unignored and indispensable, 35

Of all men I most resemble Ādam—peace be on him—while my father, Ibrāhīm—peace be on him—most resembled me in form and character, 60
One of you is in the Fire; its molar tooth is as (big as) Uḥud, 66
Only what was exposed of him to the sun and the wind was of a reddish hue, such as his face and neck, whereas what was covered by his clothing was luminous in tone, free from any reddish tint, 58

The Prophet—God bless him and grant him peace—was sparse in speech and sparse in conversation. When he commanded the people to battle he would set to work briskly with thorough preparation and he would be the most intrepid of people, 51

Rather, I eat as a slave eats, and I sit as a slave sits, 54

The seal on the letter is better than insinuation, 39
Sometimes I saw him leading us in the noon prayer attired in a cloak the two ends of which he had tied into a knot, 39
Such is indeed Satan's way of eating, 32

Take it easy, for I am not a king. I am only the son of a woman of Quraysh who used to eat dried meat, 54
There is nothing with me, but make a purchase on my credit and when something comes our way we will pay for it…, 50
These mosques are not appropriate for such defilement, whether urination or excretion, 47
There is no Muslim who clothes another Muslim with what is worn out of his garments—and he does so only for God's sake—except that he is within God's security, refuge and goodness as long as the garment covers him whilst living or deceased, 40
They said that God's Messenger—God bless him and grant him peace—did not reproach any believer except that it was made an atonement and a mercy for him, 21
This food is indeed wholesome, 32
Trustworthy, chosen one, inviting to goodness, Like the light of the full moon dispelling darkness, 58
Two drinks in one drink and two victuals in one dish?, 36

Verily, God has enfolded Islām with the nobilities of ethical character and the refinements of good works, 10
Verily he witnessed (the battle of) Badr, and, for all you know, perhaps God, Mighty, Majestic, has regarded the partisans of Badr and said: Do what you will, for I have forgiven you, 45
Verily I am a slave; I eat as a slave eats, and I sit as a slave sits, 31
Verily she is afflicted with leprosy…. Let her then be so, 68

We most certainly do not seek to attain to victory with the assistance of polytheists, 15
When the pressure intensified and each party confronted the other, we defended ourselves by the Messenger of God—God bless him and grant him peace—for there was none in more proximity to the enemy than him, 51
Who will defend you against me?, 44
Woe to you! Who will act justly if I don't act justly? I would fail and be in loss if I did not act justly, 43
Woe to you! Who will show you justice after me?, 43

You have surely seen me at the battle of Badr while we were taking refuge with the Prophet—God bless him and grant him peace. He was the nearest of us to the enemy and the most forceful of people that day in his intrepidity, 51

Index of People

ʿAbd al-Muṭṭalib, 52
Abū al-Bakhtarī, 21
Abū Bakr al-Ṣiddīq, 58
Abū Burdah bin Nayyār, 10
Abū Ṭalhah, 62
Abū Ṭālib, 57
Ādam (the Prophet), 60
Aḥmad (Prophet Muḥammad), 60
ʿĀʾishah, 7, 27, 33, 54
ʿAlī ibn Abī Ṭālib, 9, 39, 44, 49, 51, 68, 69
ʿĀmir ibn al-Ṭufayl ibn Mālik, 66
ʿAmmār ibn Yāsir, 64
Anas ibn Mālik, 11, 22, 44, 63
Arbad ibn Qays, 66
al-Aswad al-ʿAnsī, 65

Bashīr, 63
Bilāl, 43

Chosroes, 65

Fatimah bint Muḥammad (Prophet's daughter), 67
al-Ḥakam ibn Abī al-ʿĀs, 68
al-Ḥasan ibn ʿAlī (Prophet's grandson), 64
Ḥāṭib ibn Abī Baltaʿah, 45
Ḥātim al-Ṭayyiʾi, 10, 69

Ibn ʿĀmir, 53
(ʿAbdullāh) Ibn Masʿūd, 68

Ibrāhīm (the Prophet), 60
ʿImrān ibn Ḥuṣayn, 51

Jābir, 43
Jibrīl (the Archangel), 25, 27, 44

al-Miqdād, 45
Muʿādh ibn Jabal, 10, 11
Mūsā (the Prophet), 46

Qutham, 60

Saʿd ibn Hishām, 7
Shabīb ibn al-Barṣāʾ, 69
Surāqah (ibn Mālik) ibn Juʿsham, 65

Ubayy ibn Khalaf al-Jumaḥī, 66
Umm Maʿbad al-Khuzāʿiyyah, 68
Umm Salamah, 39
ʿUmar ibn al-Khattab, 45, 43, 45, 50, 63
ʿUthmān ibn ʿAffān, 32, 64

Yūnus (the Prophet), 33

Zaynab bint Jaḥsh al-Asadiyyah, 67
Zubayr, 44

Index of Places

Andalusia, 67
Badr, 45, 51, 67
The Earth, 70
the East, 67, 70
Hudaybiyah, 63
Ḥunayn, 43, 50
Khaybar, 68
the Levant, 22
Makkah, 22, 45
the North, 67
Rawḍat Khākh
Sanʿāʾ, 65
the South, 67
Ṭābah (Madīnah), 22
Tabūk, 63
Uḥud, 8, 66
the West, 67, 70
Yemen, 65

Index of Subjects

ʿ*abāʿah*, 40
ablution, 22, 41, 63
al-ʿAḍbāʾ, 41
admonishment, 29
the Afterlife, 11, 19, 54
Age of Ignorance, 55
ʿ*ajwah* dates, 34
allotments, 45
alms-giving, 67
angels, 62
anger, 47
the Anti-Christ, 29
apostate, 66
the Arabs, 10, 61, 50, 62
armomancy, 65
army, 63
the Assembler, 60
ʿ*ātiq*, 36
atonement, 21
attire, 37
augury, 65
averting of the gaze, 47
azhar, 57

barley, 15, 63
battles, 40, 44, 45, 50, 51, 66, 68
beasts of burden, 40
Bedouin, 29, 47, 48
benevolence, 17
the Berbers, 67
birds, 33
blood money, 15
bondsman, 18
bondswoman, 18
bow, 41
bravery (of the Prophet), 51-53
bread, 15, 29, 34, 35, 63
butter, 32, 34

camels, 15, 17, 18, 41, 48, 50, 53, 63
children, 22, 41, 53
cleansing-vessel, 41
cloak, 16, 17, 38, 39, 50
clothing, 16, 18, 37
coins, 50
the Community, 67
Companions (of the Prophet), 15, 18, 23, 24, 28, 43, 44, 46, 47, 48, 53, 54, 64, 65, 68
Companionship, 49
comportment, 21
conversation, 27, 51
cooking pot, 32, 34
council, 24
cucumbers, 32

ḍafaf, 31
dates, 15, 32, 63

Dhū al-Fiqār, 40
dinar, 13
dirham, 13, 50
the Ditch (battle of), 63
divination, 64
doing good, 47, 48
donkey, 17, 41, 53
drink, 35, 36
al-Duldul, 41

eating, 32
the Effacer, 60
Emigrants, 45
endive, 34
enemy, 51
ethical character, 7, 62
ethical comportment, 7, 62

falsehood, 30, 52
felt, 38
the Fire, 65
food, 18, 31, 33, 34, 35, 36, 62, 68
forgiveness (of the Prophet), 43
Friday prayer, 40
fruits, 32
funerals, 16, 38

the Garden, 31, 34
garlic, 34
garment, 37, 39
generosity, 11, 49
generosity (of the Prophet), 49-50
gifts, 14
goats, 49, 63
gold, 43
gourds, 33, 34
grapes, 32, 33
guidance, 30

habit, 16
headcloth, 39
the Hereafter, 33
honey, 15, 32, 36
household, 36
household chores, 14
howdah, 45
humankind, 16
humility, 36, 53
humility (of the Prophet), 53-55
hunger, 15
huwayna, 60

ᶜĪnah, 41
Injīl (Gospel). 22
al-ᶜIqāb, 40

jamrah, 53
Jewish man/woman, 44,
the Jews, 64
jurists, 61
justice, 11

al-Kāfūr, 41
katif, 65
al-Katūm, 41
kinsfolk, 17
knowledge, 62

language, 27
the Last, 60
the Last Hour, 29
laughter, 27
leather, 40

magnanimity, 11
mat, 40, 50
meat, 15, 29, 33, 35
melons, 16, 32
Messenger of Battles, 60
Messenger of Mercy, 60
Messenger of Repentance, 60
al-Mikhdam, 40
milk, 16, 18, 33, 36, 41, 68
miracles (of the Prophet), 61, 62
miracles (of the Qur'an), 69
moon, 62
moral character, 22, 61, 62
mosques, 47

mountain balm, 34
mudd, 63
mule, 17, 41
munificence, 49
musk, 58
Muslim, 40
mutton, 44
mutual imprecation (*mubāhalah*), 66

nobilities of character, 7, 10, 18

onions, 34
orchards, 18

paedonymies, 24
Paradise, 64
pastimes, 18
patience, 46
pearls, 58
physique (of the Prophet), 59
pleasant converse, 10
pleasure, 47
poison, 34
polytheists, 15, 45, 52
prophecy, 62
prophets, 60
provisioning of food, 10
provisions, 50
praiseworthy manners, 18
pumpkins, 33
purslane, 34

al-Qaḍīb, 41
qalansuwah, 17
al-Qaṣwāʾ, 41
the Quraysh, 54, 62, 65, 67

Ramaḍān, 49
reckoning, 36
refinement of character, 7, 9
responsibility, 49
Revealed Law, 61
Revelation, 62
al-rijlah, 34
ring, 39
robe, 37
al-Rusūb, 41

saffron, 38
sages, 61
salt, 32
Satan, 32
seal, 39
Seal of Prophethood, 57, 58, 59
self-importance, 16
sermon, 29
sheep, 32, 34
shirt, 37, 38
signet ring, 17
silver, 16, 40, 41, 43
slaves, 14, 17, 22, 31, 38, 53
smile, 29
sorcery, 34
soup, 33
speech, 27, 49, 51
spell, 44
squadron, 52
starvation, 29
the Successor, 60
sugar, 32
sweet-dish, 15
sweetmeat, 32
sword, 40, 41, 44

(the clan of) Ṭayyiʾ, 10
thorn-tail lizard, 35
tree, 33
truth, 30
truthfulness (of the Prophet), 61
tunic, 37, 38, 40
turban, 17, 39
the Turks, 67

valor, 52
vanity, 36
vegetables, 34
victuals, 36
vinegar, 34

virtuous conduct, 12
visitor, 23, 24

waist-wrapper, 37, 38
water, 33, 35, 41, 63
weapons, 40
wedding feasts, 16
wheat, 15, 32
wisdom teeth, 29
wives (of the Prophet), 18
woolen gown, 16
womenfolk, 14, 22
worldly life, 19
worshipper, 31

Ya'fūr, 41
yellow color, 47
Yemeni striped-cloth, 16

zajr, 65

About the Translator

Dr. ʿAdī Setia

Dr. ʿAdī Setia (adisetiawangsa@gmail.com) taught Islamic Science and Islamic Economics at the Center for Advanced Studies on Islam, Science & Civilization (CASIS), Malaysia. He was a Research Fellow at ISTAC, Malaysia, under the guidance of Professor Syed Muhammad Naquib al-Attas. He has also studied for some years at traditional Malay-Islamic madrasahs in Malaysia and Patani. His research interests are mainly in History and Philosophy of Science, Islamic Science, Islamic Gift Economy (IGE), and Islamization of Knowledge according to the integrative conceptual framework of al-Attas. His papers in these areas are mostly published in the Canadian journal Islamic Sciences (http://www.cis-ca.org/islamscience1.php). He previously translated Book 13 of the *Ihya'* as *The Book of the Proprieties of Earning and Living* (Kuala Lumpur: IBFIM, 2013).

About the Author of the Preface

Dr. Walead Muhammad Mosaad

Dr. Walead Muhammad Mosaad is the Chair and Scholar-in-Residence of Sabeel Community. Additionally, he is the director of Muslim student life at Lehigh University. He has also participated in the Traveling Light Series on Imam al-Ghazālī, and is an advisor on the Fons Vitae Ghazālī children's series of books. He has completed degrees from Rutgers University, Fath Islamic Seminary in Damascus, Al-Azhar University in Cairo, the University of Liverpool, and a PhD in Arab and Islamic Studies at the University of Exeter in the UK. His studies and work have afforded him the opportunity to travel across much of the Muslim world, studying the Islamic tradition with several scholars of our time.

About the Author of the Foreword

Dr. Afifi al-Akiti

Shaykh Dato' Dr. Afifi al-Akiti is the KFAS (Kuwait Foundation for the Advancement of Science) Fellow in Islamic Studies at the Oxford Centre for Islamic Studies and Lecturer in Islamic Studies in the Faculty of Theology, Oxford University. His areas of expertise are Islamic theology, philosophy and science. He was educated originally at the feet of the ulama of the Muslim world, and in 2010 was made a Member of the Ulama Council by the Ruler of Perak, Malaysia, HRH Sultan Nazrin Shah. Since 2010, he has been listed in *The Muslim 500: The World's 500 Most Influential Muslims.*

About the Author of the Introduction

Shaykh Muhammad ibn Yahya ibn Ali al-Ninowy

Shaykh Muhammad ibn Yahya ibn Ali al-Ninowy, whose lineage is traced back to the Prophet Muḥammad through his grandson, Hussein Ibn Alī, received his PhD in Hadith Sciences at Al-Azhar University. An accomplished and recognized scholar of traditional Islamic religious sciences, he also studied in Syria, Mecca, Madina, Morocco, and other countries. He is the author of numerous books on various aspects of Islam and travels worldwide promoting peace and understanding amongst people. He is the Founding Director of the Medina Institutes, which offer Islamic Studies degrees geared towards educating imams and theological scholars.